D1593881

A Turning Point for Europe?

JOSEPH CARDINAL RATZINGER

A TURNING POINT FOR EUROPE?

The Church in the Modern World—
Assessment and Forecast

Translated by
Brian McNeil, C.R.V.

IGNATIUS PRESS   SAN FRANCISCO

Title of the German original:
Wendezeit für Europa?
Diagnosen und Prognosen zur Lage von Kirche und Welt
© 1991 Johannes Verlag, Einsiedeln

Cover by Roxanne Mei Lum

Contents

Part One

Foundations and Fundamental Questions in Relation to the Church and the Modern World

PART TWO

Assessment and Forecast

Preface

When one looks back at the history of our century, it is very easy to discern three great turning points that have affected initially and immediately the structure of life in Europe, but all three have also affected and continue to affect the history of the world as a whole. First, we must mention the transformation of the external and internal map of Europe that resulted from the First World War. It brought with it the collapse of the monarchies in central Europe, the end of Czarist Russia and the restructuring of the whole of Europe in keeping with the nationalist principle—which, of course, on closer inspection proved externally impracticable and inherently insufficient as the foundation of a new order of peace. The Second World War was followed by the partition of Europe and of the world into two mutually opposed power blocs: the Marxist and the liberal capitalist. Now, at the end of the century, we have experienced the internal disintegration of Marxist ideology together with the structure of power it had created. The special characteristic of this third turning point is that it took place without a war and almost without any bloodshed, simply through the internal collapse of a system and its intellectual foundations, that is, through the powers of the spirit and not through military or political force. Herein lie both the hope and the special responsibility of this event, and we are still very far from meeting the challenge it poses.

Liberalism and Marxism were in agreement in refusing religion both the right and the capacity to shape public affairs and the common future of mankind. In the maturation process of the second half of this century, religion has been discovered anew as an ineradicable force both of individual and of social living. It has become clear that one cannot plan and shape the future of mankind while prescinding from religion. This process gives comfort to faith, but faith will not fail to recognize at the same time the dangers inherent in it, for the temptation is obvious on all sides to take in religion as an instrument to serve political ideas. In this situation it is an absolute obligation for the theologian and for the pastor of the Church to enter the dispute about the correct understanding of the present time and about the path into the future, in order both to clarify faith's own proper sphere and at the same time to fulfill his own share of responsibility at this hour. I have been invited with increasing frequency in recent years to speak on themes concerning the relationship of the Church and the world; most of these were formulated by those who issued the invitation, thus giving expression to questions perceived to be especially urgent at each particular place. I have collected in this little book the more important studies that arose in this manner. After the wide response they have found in audiences in a great variety of places, I venture to hope that they have something to say both to believers and to doubters and that they can help in meeting the challenges of the present hour in our history.

JOSEPH CARDINAL RATZINGER
Rome, Easter 1991

ACKNOWLEDGMENTS

Note on first publication of the essays in this book

"Breaking down and Starting out Afresh: Faith's Answer to the Crisis of Values": "Abbruch und Aufbruch. Die Antwort des Glaubens auf die Krise der Werte", *Eichstätter Hochschulreden* 61 (Munich, 1988).

"Peace and Justice in Crisis: The Task of Religion": "Der Auftrag der Religion angesichts der gegenwärtigen Krise von Friede und Gerechtigkeit", *Internat. kath. Zeitschrift* 18 (1989), 113–22.

"Faith and Social Responsibility": "Glaube und soziale Verantwortung": hitherto unpublished.

"Paths of Faith in the Revolutionary Change of the Present Day": "Wege des Glaubens im Umbruch der Gegenwart": hitherto unpublished in German.

"Europe—Hopes and Dangers": "Europa—Hoffnungen und Gefahren", published as a pamphlet, Speyer, 1990.

"A Turning Point for Europe?": "Wendezeit für Europa?", published in *Deutsche Tagespost; Die Presse* (Vienna); *KNA ökumenische Information* Nr. 14/15 (1991), 5–16.

PART ONE

FOUNDATIONS AND FUNDAMENTAL
QUESTIONS IN RELATION TO
THE CHURCH AND
THE MODERN WORLD

I

BREAKING DOWN
AND STARTING OUT AFRESH:
FAITH'S ANSWER TO THE CRISIS OF VALUES

The image of man that dominates in modern litera-
ture, in visual arts, cinema and theater is primarily a
gloomy image. The great and the noble are suspect
from the outset; they must be torn from their pedes-
tal so that one can see through them. Morality counts
as hypocrisy, joy as self-deception. Anyone who simply puts trust in the beautiful and the good is either
inexcusably ingenuous or acting with evil intent. The
truly moral attitude is suspicion, and its greatest success is in exposing. Criticism of society is obligatory;
it is impossible to find words lurid and brutal enough
to describe the dangers that threaten us. This delight
in the negative is not, however, unlimited. There
exists at the same time an obligation to be optimistic,
and the failure to observe this obligation does not go
unpunished. For example, anyone who expresses the
view that not everything in the intellectual development of the modern period has been correct, that it
is necessary in some essential areas to reflect on the

shared wisdom of the great cultures, has chosen to make the wrong kind of criticism. He finds himself suddenly confronted with a resolute *apologia* for the fundamental decisions of the modern age; no matter how much delight one may take in negation, he is not permitted to call into question the view that the fundamental trajectory of historical development is progress and that the good lies in the future—and nowhere else.

The strange schizophrenia of today's criticism of society becomes palpably clear in the radically contradictory ways in which dominant opinion has reacted to the two events that were perceived recently to be the strongest moral challenges to our society. The first of these was the disaster at Chernobyl. If one wished to appear enlightened, one could not find words drastic enough to portray the danger of what had happened. One had to see a monstrous threat hanging over every living creature, and the only sufficient response could be the total abandonment of atomic energy. The second event was the rapid advance of the new viral illness AIDS. There can be no doubt that many more people will become sick and die (or have already died) of AIDS than of the consequences of Chernobyl and that the risk caused by this new scourge of mankind stands much nearer to the door of each individual than the risk caused by nuclear power plants. But anyone who dares to say that mankind should set itself free from the chaotic

sexual libertinism that gives AIDS its offensive poten-
tial is dismissed by public opinion as a hopeless
obscurantist: such an idea can only be deplored by
one's enlightened contemporaries, who pass over it
in silence. All this shows us that there exists today a
permissible criticism of society and a forbidden criticism of society; but the permissible criticism goes
only as far as the threshold of fundamental decisions,
which may not be called into question.

1. THE MORAL PROBLEMS OF OUR AGE—
AN ATTEMPT AT A DIAGNOSIS

The theme proposed here naturally demands a reflection that does not allow itself to be intimidated by
such prohibitions. Nevertheless, it would be wrong,
conversely, to see our society and its moral situation
as a whole only in tones of unrelieved gray. We must
not let ourselves be affected by the superficial obligatory optimism of certain trends, but, equally, we
must not yield to the temptation to overlook the
positive elements in the total complex of our age. It
is, of course, not possible here to give an exhaustive
description of the moral physiognomy of our age.
The aim of our reflections is to find support and
healing, that fundamental orientation with which to
survive the present and thus open the path into the
future. We are inquiring about the characteristic ele-

ments of *our* age, in order to recognize what hinders and what serves access to the correct path. Thus, in this first part of our analysis, we are not discussing defects or virtues that have always existed and no doubt always will exist but rather characteristic signs of our own times. In a negative perspective, there are two striking elements here that do not belong in the same way to other periods: terrorism and drugs. On the positive side, a strong moral consciousness is being asserted, concentrating essentially on values of the social sphere: freedom for the oppressed, solidarity with the poor and disadvantaged, peace and reconciliation.

a. The Problem of Drugs

Let us attempt to look somewhat more closely at these phenomena. I recall a debate I had with some friends in Ernst Bloch's house. Our conversation chanced to hit on the problem of drugs, which at that time—in the late 1960s—was just beginning to arise. We wondered how this temptation could spread so suddenly now, and why, for example, it had apparently not existed at all in the Middle Ages. All were agreed in rejecting as insufficient the answer that at that period the areas where drugs were cultivated were too far away. Phenomena like the appearance of drugs are not to be explained by means of such external conditions; they come from deeper

needs or lacks, while dealing with the concrete problems of procurement follows later. I ventured the
hypothesis that obviously in the Middle Ages the
emptiness of the soul, which drugs are an attempt to
fill, did not exist: the thirst of the soul, of the inner
man, found an answer that made drugs unnecessary. I
can still recall the speechless indignation with which
Mrs. Bloch reacted to this proposed solution. On the
basis of dialectical materialism's image of history, she
found the idea almost criminal that past ages could
have been superior to our own in not wholly ines-
sential matters; it was impossible that the masses
could have lived with greater happiness and inner
harmony in the Middle Ages—a period of oppression
and religious prejudices—than in our age, which has
already made some degree of progress along the path
of liberation: this would entail the collapse of the
entire logic of "liberation". But how, then, is one to
explain what has happened? The question remained
unanswered that evening.

Since I do not share the materialistic image of the
world, I continue to believe that my thesis was correct. Naturally, however, it must be made more concrete, and it is precisely the thinking of Ernst Bloch
that can offer a helpful starting point here. For Bloch,
the world of facts is a bad world. The principle of
hope means that man energetically contradicts the
facts; he knows he is obliged to overcome the bad
world of facts in order to create a better world. I

would put it in this way: drugs are a form of protest against facts. The one who takes them refuses to resign himself to the world of facts. He seeks a better world. Drugs are the result of despair in a world experienced as a dungeon of facts, in which man cannot hold out for long. Naturally, many other things are involved, too: the search for adventure; the conformity of joining in what others are doing; the cleverness of the dealers, and so on. But the core is a protest against a reality perceived as a prison. The "great journey" that men attempt in drugs is the perversion of mysticism, the perversion of the human need for infinity, the rejection of the impossibility of transcending immanence, and the attempt to extend the limits of one's own existence into the infinite. The patient and humble adventure of asceticism, which, in small steps of ascent, comes closer to the descending God, is replaced by magical power, the magical key of drugs—the ethical and religious path is replaced by technology. Drugs are the pseudo-mysticism of a world that does not believe yet cannot get rid of the soul's yearning for paradise. Thus, drugs are a warning sign that points to [something] very profound: not only do they disclose a vacuum in our society, which that society's own instruments cannot fill, but they also point to an inner claim of man's nature, a claim that asserts itself in a perverted form if it does not find the correct answer.

b. Terrorism as a Moral Problem

Terrorism's point of departure is closely related to that of drugs: here, too, we find at the outset a protest against the world as it is and the desire for a better world. On the basis of its roots, terrorism is a moralism, albeit a misdirected one that becomes the brutal parody of the true aims and paths of morality. It is not by chance that terrorism had its beginning in the universities, and here once again in the milieu of modern theology, in young people who at the outset were strongly influenced by religion. Terrorism was at first a religious enthusiasm that had been redirected into the earthly realm, a messianic expectation transposed into political fanaticism. Faith in life after death had broken down, or at least had become irrelevant, but the criterion of heavenly expectation was not abandoned: rather, it was now applied to the present world. God was no longer seen as one who genuinely acts, but the fulfillment of his promises was demanded just as it had always been, and, indeed, with a new vigor. "God has no other arms but ours"—this now meant that the fulfillment of these promises can and must be carried out by ourselves. Disgust at the intellectual and spiritual emptiness of our society, yearning for what is completely different, the claim to unconditional salvation without restrictions and without limits—this is, so to speak, the religious component in the phenomenon of terrorism, which gives it the impetus of a passion focused on a totality, its uncompromising character and the claim to be idealistic. All this becomes so dangerous because of the decisively earthly character of the messianic hope: something unconditional is demanded of what is conditional, something infinite is demanded of what is finite. This inherent contradiction indicates the real tragedy of this phenomenon in which man's great vocation becomes the instrument of the great lie.

The false dimension in terrorism's promise was, however, concealed, as far as the average participant was concerned, by connecting the religious expectation to modern intellectuality. This means, first, that all traditional moral criteria are dragged before the tribunal of positivistic reason, "called into question" and "seen through" as unproven. Morality does not lie in Being but in the future. Man must devise it himself. The sole moral value that exists is the future society in which everything that does not exist now will be fulfilled. Thus morality in the present consists in working for this future society. Accordingly, the new moral criterion states: "Moral" is what serves to bring about the new society. What serves to do this, however, can be ascertained with the scientific methods of political strategy, with psychology and with sociology. Morality becomes "scientific": its goal is no longer a "phantom"—heaven—but a phenomenon that can be constructed, the new age. Thus the moral and the religious have become realistic and "scientific". What more could one want? Is it any wonder that it was precisely idealistic young people who felt challenged by these promises?

It is only on closer inspection that one sees the cloven hoof in its entirety and hears Mephistopheles sneering. " 'Moral' is whatever creates the future": on this criterion, even murder can be "moral"; even the inhuman must serve on the path to humanity. Fundamentally, this is the same logic as that which says that even embryos may be sacrificed for "genuinely high-quality scientific results". And the concept of freedom here is the same as that which teaches us that it must be a part of a woman's freedom to get rid of a child that stands in the way of her self-realization. Thus terrorism moves on today, without any restriction, to somewhat more elevated battle-fields, with the full blessing of science and of the enlightened human intellect. Certainly the coarse terrorism of those who would change society has been brought under control in Western societies: it has been too great a threat to the accustomed life of these societies, and the immorality of its morality has become too obvious. But a genuine dissociation from its foundations has still not taken place; one sign of this is the fact that terrorism is still recommended without any embarrassment to Third World countries that lie sufficiently far removed from us. Today, just as earlier on, one is regarded as virtually immoral if one fails to praise slogans for the Third World that one would not like to see applied in one's own surroundings. Taking the side of militant ideologies of liberation seems a kind of moral compensation for accepting a comfortable life in which one wants to see nothing essential changed. We can thank God that the praxis of terrorism has been reduced in Europe, but its intellectual foundations have not been overcome, and, until this happens, its flames can be kindled anew at any time.

c. The New Turning to Morality and Religion

We are now confronted very emphatically with the question: What is it that is really false in these intellectual foundations that we have only sketched briefly here? Exactly where does the error lie? Before we examine this question in depth, we must complete our inventory of today's society. We have said that the outstanding negative phenomena are the advances made by drugs and the threat posed by terrorism; but there also exists, as a positive phenomenon, a strong new will to work for great moral values like freedom, justice and peace. Can this perhaps supply the answer to the threats that hang over our age? We must begin by noting that the values that have the greatest prominence here are largely identical with those that have been and are proclaimed as well by the supporters of violent movements as the values at which they aim. But this misuse does not discredit the values as such. What is new in many of the young generation of today is the fact that these goals are now projected onto the level of concrete political and social action and thereby stripped of their irrational and violent character. The ideologies are cut away, so that it becomes possible to see the good in its purity once again. One may in truth call this an element of hope: the deep divine message in man can be buried and disfigured, but it breaks out again and again and creates a path for itself. In this context, we must also note that a new desire for recollection, for contemplation, for true sacrality, indeed, for contact with God is perceptible.

Thus forces are emerging that permit us to hope. But just as the spring of water must be contained to prevent it from drying up, so these impulses, too, need to be purified and given structure, so that they can have their true effect. The new religious interest can very easily be diverted into the esoteric; it can evaporate into mere romanticism. It is extremely difficult for this religious interest to leap over two hurdles: it seems to be difficult to accept the continuity of a steady discipline, of a straight path that does not allow itself to be diverted from the ordering of the will and of the reason into quick satisfactions through techniques based on feelings. But it seems to be even more difficult to lead such a religious interest into the context of the common life of an "institution" of faith in which religion, as faith, has become the form and path of a community. But where this double hurdle is not surmounted, religion degenerates into a luxury; it does not develop any binding moral force for the community or for the individual. Understanding and the will disappear from religion; all that remains is feeling alone, and that is too little.

The new moral impulses, too, are at risk in similar ways. Their exposed flank is the general lack of individual-ethical values. The gaze is directed to the great totality, to what concerns the community. Certainly, one must acknowledge that the attention paid to marginalized groups often finds expression, too, in a personal readiness to help, which gives rise to the motivation to serve and to give assistance in admirable ways. But on the whole, one observes, rather, a weakness in personal motivating force. It is easier to demonstrate for the rights and freedoms of one's own group than to practice in daily living the discipline of freedom and the patience of love for those who suffer, or, indeed, to bind oneself to such service for the whole of one's life, with the concomitant renunciation of a great part of one's own individual freedoms. It is noticeable that the motivating force to serve in the Church, too, has clearly become decisively weaker: there are scarcely any vocations now for Orders that dedicate themselves to caring for the sick and the elderly. One prefers to work in more "pastorally"

ambitious services. But what is in fact more truly
"pastoral" than the unpretentious existence at the
service of those who suffer? No matter how important the professional qualification for these services is,
without a deep moral and religious foundation, they
congeal into mere technology and no longer perform
what is critical in human terms.

Thus, the weak side of today's moral awakening
lies first of all in the weakness of the individual-
ethical motivating force. But something deeper lies
behind this: moral values have lost their evidential
character, and thus also their compelling claim, in a
society conditioned by technology. They indicate
goals for the totality, goals that awaken enthusiasm
and zeal; but it is not clear to me why they should
continue to be obligatory when this has negative
consequences for me, threatening my own freedom
and my personal peace. But this means that these
goals remain largely ineffective, and the public vigor
with which they are proclaimed in demonstrations
and continually defended in speeches is surely itself a
compensation for this lack of concrete effectiveness.
So this brings us once again to the question that we
left unanswered above: Where precisely is the beginning of the error in that kind of moralism that ends
in terrorism? For this error is the real root of almost
all the other problems of our epoch; its practical consequences extend far beyond the areas affected by terrorism.

2. ELEMENTS OF AN ANSWER

a. The Essence of What Is Moral

Let us try to feel our way slowly toward the facts of the case. I said that that which is moral has lost its evidential character. Only a small number of people in modern society still believe in the existence of divine commandments, and still fewer are convinced that these commandments—if they exist—are communicated to us without error through the Church, through the religious community. The idea that another will, the will of the Creator, calls us and that our being is right when our will is in harmony with his will is an idea that is foreign to most people. The only function remaining for God at best is that of having set the primal Big Bang in motion; the notion that he is actively present in our midst and that man is subject to his will seems to most people a naively anthropomorphic concept of God in which man overestimates himself. The idea of a personal relationship between the Creator God and each individual person is certainly not wholly absent in the religious and ethical history of man, but in its pure form it is limited to the sphere of biblical religion. But there is an objective connection between this and the conviction that was common to almost the whole of mankind before the modern period, the conviction that

man's Being contains an imperative; the conviction
that he does not himself *invent* morality on the basis
of calculations of expediency but rather *finds* it
already present in the essence of things. Long before
the outbreak of terrorism and the invasion by drugs,
the English author and philosopher C. S. Lewis
pointed to the fatal danger of the abolition of man
that lies in the collapse of the foundations of our
morality, emphasizing the evidential character of
mankind as a whole on which the existence of man
qua man rests. He reviews all the great cultures to
show the existence of this evidential character. Not
only does he refer to the moral inheritance of the
Greeks, as this was articulated especially by Plato,
Aristotle and the Stoics, who wish to lead man to
perceive the rationality of Being and, therefore,
demand an education in "connaturality with reason";
he recalls also the idea of *Rta* in early Hinduism,
which speaks of the harmony of the cosmic order,
the moral virtues and the ceremonial of the temple.
He emphasizes especially the Chinese teaching of the
Tao: "It is Nature, it is the Way, the Road. It is the
Way in which the universe goes on. . . . It is also the
Way which every man should tread in imitation of
that cosmic and supercosmic progression, conforming
all activities to that great exemplar."[1] But Lewis also

[1] C. S. Lewis, *The Abolition of Man, or Reflections on Education
with Special Reference to the Teaching of English in the Upper Forms of
Schools* (New York, 1947), 28.

refers to the law of Israel, which links cosmos and history and intends to be an expression of the truth of man as well as of the truth of the world as a whole. There are differences in detail within this knowledge shared by the great cultures, but stronger than the differences is the great common area that presents itself as the primal evidential character of human life: the doctrine of objective values expressed in the Being of the world; the belief that attitudes exist that correspond to the message of the universe and are true and therefore good, and that other attitudes likewise exist that are genuinely and always false because they contradict Being.

Men in the modern period have been persuaded that the moralities of mankind contradict each other radically, just as the religions do. In both cases, the simple conclusion has been drawn that all of this is a human construction, whose inconsistencies we now at last see through and can replace with rational knowledge. But this diagnosis is extremely superficial. It clings to a series of details that are lined up alongside each other in no particular order and thus arrives at its banal know-it-all attitude. In reality, the fundamental intuition about the moral character of Being itself and about the necessary harmony between the human being and the message of nature is common to all the great cultures, and therefore the great moral imperatives are likewise held in common. C. S. Lewis has stated this emphatically:

This thing which I have called for convenience the *Tao*, and which others may call Natural Law or Traditional Morality or the First Principles of Practical Reason or the First Platitudes, is not one among a series of possible systems of value. It is the sole source of all value judgements. If it is rejected, all value is rejected. If any value is retained, it is retained. The effort to refute it and raise a new system of value in its place is self-contradictory.[2]

b. The Falsification of Scientism: The Abolition of Man

The problem of the modern period, that is, the moral problem of our age, consists in the fact that it has separated itself from this primal evidential character. In order genuinely to understand this process, we must describe it still more precisely. It is characteristic of thought marked by the natural sciences to posit a gulf between the world of feelings and the world of facts. Feelings are subjective, facts are objective. "Facts", that is, that which can be established as existing outside ourselves, are as yet only "facts", naked facticity. It belongs to the world of pure fable to attribute any qualities of a moral or aesthetic nature to the atom beyond its mathematical determinations. But the consequence of this reduction of nature to facts that can be completely grasped and therefore controlled is that no moral message

[2] Lewis, 56.

outside ourselves can now come to us. Morality, just
like religion, now belongs to the realm of the subjective; it has no place in the objective. If it is subjective, then it is something posited by man. It does not
precede vis-à-vis us: we precede it and fashion it.
This movement of "objectification", which permits
us to "see through" things and to control them,
essentially knows no limits. Auguste Comte called
for a physics of man: gradually, even the most difficult object of nature—man—must become
scientifically comprehensible, that is, subordinate to
the knowledge of the natural sciences. Thus one
would see through man in precisely the same way as
one has already seen through matter.[3] Psychoanalysis
and sociology are the fundamental ways to fulfill this
demand. One can now (so it seems) explain the
mechanisms whereby man came to believe that
nature expresses a moral law. Naturally, the man
who has been "seen through" is no longer a man at
all—it belongs to the essence of such knowledge that
he, too, can be only pure facticity now: "If you see
through everything, then everything is transparent.
But a wholly transparent world is an invisible

[3] Cf. H. de Lubac, *Le Drame de l'humanisme athée*, 4th ed.
(Paris: Éd. Spes, 1950), 137–278; Eng. trans.: *The Drama of Atheist
Humanism* (Cleveland: World Pub. Co., 1950), 77–159. H. U.
von Balthasar, *Die Gottesfrage des heutigen Menschen* (Vienna,
1956); Eng. trans.: *The God Question and Modern Man* (New
York: Seabury Press, 1967).

world", writes Lewis.[4] The theories of evolution,
developed into a universal view of the world, con-
firm this optic and attempt at the same time to compensate for it.[5] Naturally (so they say), everything has
become what it is without any logic or, more correctly, through the sheer logic of facts. But it is now
possible to reconstruct this purely mechanical origin
of the world's coming into being in theories about
chance and necessity, in the perfect doctrine of evolution. The consequences drawn from "evolution",
imitations of its successes, would then be the new
morality: the goal of evolution is the survival and the
optimization of the species. The optimal survival of
the genus "man" would now be the fundamental
moral value; the rules for accomplishing this would
be the only moral regulations. It is only in appearance that this is a return to listening to the moral
instruction that nature gives: in reality, it is now the
god Meaningless who rules, for evolution on its own
terms is meaningless. Calculation rules, and power
rules. Morality has surrendered, and man *qua* man
has surrendered. It no longer makes sense to cling to
the survival of this particular species. Let us listen to

[4] Lewis, 91.

[5] Cf. on this, R. Spaemann, R. Löw, P. Koslowski, *Evolutionis-
mus und Christentum* (Acta humaniora, VCH, 1986); W. Bröker,
"Schöpfung als Auftrag", in W. Baier et al., *Weisheit Gottes—
Weisheit der Welt*, Festschrift für J. Ratzinger, 2 (St. Ottilien,
1987), 115–26.

C. S. Lewis once again. Already in 1943, he described this process with razor-sharp acuteness:

> It is the magician's bargain: give up our soul, get
> power in return. But once our souls, that is, our
> selves, have been given up, the power thus con-
> ferred will not belong to us. . . . It is in Man's power
> to treat himself as a mere 'natural object'. . . . The
> real objection is that if man chooses to treat himself
> as raw material, raw material he will be.[6]

Lewis formulated these warnings during the Second
World War, because he saw the destruction of
morality as something that threatened the ability to
defend one's native land against the oncoming storm
of barbarity. But he was objective enough to add: "I
am not here thinking solely, perhaps not even
chiefly, of those who are our public enemies at the
moment. The process which, if not checked, will
abolish Man, goes on apace among Communists and
Democrats no less than among Fascists. . . ."[7] This
remark seems to me to be very important: the most
opposite modern views of the world share the same
starting point: the denial of the natural ethical law
and the reduction of the world to "mere" facts. The
measure of what they illogically retain of the old
values is variable, but they are threatened by the same
danger in their central point.

[6] Lewis, 83–84. (The first British edition of *The Abolition of
Man* was published by Oxford University Press in 1943.)

[7] Lewis, 85.

The real untruth of the world view of which drugs and terrorism are symptoms consists in the reduction of the world to facts and in the narrowing-down of reason to the perception of what is quantitative. That which is most specific to man is shoved aside into the subjective realm and thus lacks reality. The "abolition of man", which results from the attribution of absoluteness to one single mode of knowledge, at the same time clearly falsifies this world view. Man exists, and anyone who, on the strength of his own theory, has to pull man down into the sphere of a machine that is "seen through" and can be assembled lives in a constriction of perception that misses precisely what is essential. If the aim of science is the most universal knowledge possible, the knowledge most in accordance with reality, then such an absolutized form of method is the opposite of science. This means, in other words, that practical reason too, on which genuinely ethical knowledge is based, is truly reason and not merely the expression of subjective feelings without any value as evidence. We must again learn to understand that the great ethical insights of mankind are just as rational and just as true as—indeed, more true than—the experimental knowledge of the realm of the natural sciences and technology. They are more true, because they touch more deeply the essential character of Being and have a more decisive significance for the humanity of man.

c. Reason of Morality and Reason of Faith

Two consequences derive from this. The first is that moral obligation is not man's prison, from which he must liberate himself in order finally to be able to do what he wants. It is moral obligation that constitutes his dignity, and he does not become more free if he discards it: on the contrary, he takes a step backward, to the level of a machine, of a mere thing. If there is no longer any obligation to which he can and must respond in freedom, then there is no longer any realm of freedom at all. The recognition of morality is the real substance of human dignity; but one cannot recognize this without simultaneously experiencing it as an obligation of freedom. Morality is not man's prison but rather the divine element in him.

In order to present the second consequence, we must again reflect on the fundamental insight we reached earlier: practical (or moral) reason is reason in the highest sense, because it penetrates the real mystery of reality more deeply than does experimental reason. But this means that the Christian faith is not a limitation or paralysis of reason: on the contrary, it is only this faith that sets reason free to perform its own proper work. For practical reason, too, needs the confirmation of an experiment, but of one too large to be carried out in laboratories: it needs the experiment of a human existence that has stood the test, and this can come only from history that itself has stood the test. This is why practical reason was always given its place in the great context of experience and testing of holistic ethical-religious visions. And just as the natural sciences live from brilliant breakthroughs made by great individuals, so, too, these systematizations of the ethical view depend both on the experience of community and on the exceptional vision of individuals who succeeded in gaining a glimpse of the whole. The great ethical constructs of Greece, of the Near and the Far East, of which we have spoken briefly above, have lost none of their validity in the core of what they say, but today we can see them as tributaries that ultimately flow into the great river of the Christian interpretation of reality.

The ethical vision of the Christian faith is not in fact something specific to Christianity but is the synthesis of the great ethical intuitions of mankind from a new center that holds them all together. This agreement in ethical wisdom is often put forward today as an argument against the obligatory character of the commandments of God that are proclaimed in the Bible. It is argued that this agreement shows that the Bible does not possess any ethical instruction at all of its own but simply adopts the moral insights of its milieu at the time. Accordingly, only what is recognized at a specific time as reasonable has validity in morality—and thus one has already arrived at the reduction of morality to a mere calculation, that is, at the abolition of the "moral" in the proper sense of the word. It is the opposite that is true: the inner harmony of the fundamental moral instruction, which was of course developed and purified step by step, is the best proof of its validity—the best proof that it was not invented but found already in existence. Found—how? It is here that the realms of revelation and reason penetrate one another very closely. This knowledge was found, on the one side, as we have said, by those who were able to see more deeply. We call such sight, which goes beyond one's own capacity of knowledge, revelation. But that which is seen here is, in the ethical realm, essentially the moral message that lies in creation itself. For nature is not—as is asserted by a totalitarian scientism—some assemblage built up by chance and its rules of play but is rather a creation. A creation in which the *Creator Spiritus* expresses himself. This is why there are not only natural laws in the sense of physical functions: the specific natural law itself is a moral law. Creation itself teaches us how we can be human in the right way. The Christian faith, which helps us to recognize creation as creation, does not paralyze reason; it gives practical reason the life-sphere in which it can unfold. The morality that the Church teaches is not some special burden for Christians: it is the defense of man against the attempt to abolish him. If morality—as we have seen—is not the enslavement of man but his liberation, then the Christian faith is the advance post of human freedom.

I should like to add one more reflection. The Roman poet Juvenal has formulated in an unsurpassable way my concern here:

Summum crede nefas animam praeferre pudori
et propter vitam vivendi perdere causas—

"Believe that it is the worst crime to prefer your physical life to reverence and to destroy, for the sake of living, the reasons for living." This means that there are values worth dying for, because a life purchased at the cost of betraying these values is based on the betrayal of the reasons for living and is therefore a life destroyed from within. We could express what is meant here as follows: where there is no longer anything worth dying for, life is no longer worthwhile; it has lost its point. And this is not only true for the individual; a land, too, a common culture, has values that justify the commitment of one's life; if such values no longer exist, we also lose the reasons and the forces that maintain social cohesion and preserve a country as a community of life.

This brings us once more to the reflections on which we first touched in our remarks about drugs. Man needs transcendence. Immanence alone is too narrow for him. He is created for more. The denial of an afterlife led initially to a passionate glorification of life, the assertion of life at any price. For everything must be attained in this life—there is nothing else. The lust for life, the lust for all kinds of fulfillment, was intensified to the utmost. But at once, an enormous devaluation of life came from this: life is no longer surrounded by the seal of the holy; one throws it away when it no longer pleases. The misshapen triplets—abortion, euthanasia, suicide—are the natural progeny of this fundamental decision, which is the denial of eternal responsibility and of eternal hope. Lust for life changes into disgust with life and into the emptiness of its fulfillments. Here, too, the abolition of man is the consequence.

Man needs morality in order to be himself. But morality requires faith in creation and immortality, that is, it needs the objectivity of obligation and the definitiveness of responsibility and fulfillment. The impossibility of a human existence cut off from these is the indirect proof of the truth of the Christian faith and of its hope. It is this hope that saves man, today as ever—indeed, precisely today. The Christian is entitled to be glad in his faith. Without the good news of faith, human existence does not survive in the long run. The joy of faith is its responsibility: we should seize it with new courage in this hour of our history.

II

PEACE AND JUSTICE IN CRISIS: THE TASK OF RELIGION

In this paper I have been asked to speak about the present-day crisis of peace and justice and to indicate the contribution religion can make to the resolution of the problem. Now there is no such thing as religion in the abstract; it always has a concrete historical form. So my starting point will not be a general concept of religion. Instead I shall direct my questions concretely to my own faith as a Christian and a Catholic. What can our faith, in its true and original character, do to help us resolve these problems? Perhaps also, what can and must it not do if it is to remain true to what it is? To make the first half of the discussion more manageable, I would like to define the issue somewhat more narrowly and precisely. I do not intend to offer an empirical analysis of today's crisis of peace and justice in all its different facets. Given the scale of the thing, it would fill a whole book and is perhaps an impossible undertaking for one person on his own, even supposing he has more specialized knowledge and opportunities for research than I have. My intention is not descriptive but, in the broad sense of the term, normative. In other words, by looking at the actual phenomena, I want to see what peace is, what justice is, and how the two are connected, in order to understand our ethical task. However, such an analysis does not take place "within the limits of reason alone" (to use the words of Kant) but in the light of what the Christian faith can tell us about the two themes, that is to say, in an openness of reason to knowledge. Reason does not itself simply produce knowledge, and yet the knowledge, once given, is real knowledge. In this respect religion has a contribution to make in the analysis of the phenomena as well as in the highlighting of the ethical imperatives.

1. Threats to Peace—Loss of the Criteria for Justice and Injustice

Our theme links peace and justice. The crisis of the one is the crisis of the other, and vice versa. When justice begins to falter, peace falters too. In fact, one might say that wars always break out when there is no clear or compelling criterion of justice. I think this becomes evident when we consider the four ways in which peace is actually threatened in today's world.

The first threat to peace, the one that most preoccupies public awareness, is the danger of world war, the danger that the great power blocs, into which the world is divided, would unleash against each other those weapons of mass destruction that in all probability would bring about the destruction of the human race.

The second way in which peace is endangered and destroyed consists in the so-called "classical" wars. In the last forty years, in different parts of the world, these have taken place in unending succession: wars in the Middle East, in Africa, in Southeast Asia, the war between Argentina and Great Britain, and so on.

The third form might be called the state's loss of internal peace. This takes two distinct and yet interrelated forms:

The so-called liberation movements struggle for power when they regard the state's legal power as one of injustice. They see rebellion against the order of the state, a rebellion in itself destructive of peace, as a commitment to justice and thus the only way to establish peace, in fact, a duty in the cause of true peace. Interestingly, a large number of those people who consider themselves to be pacifists with regard to the first type of war (world war) look upon this other form of struggle, often very cruel and bloody, as something really sacred, a higher form of the *bellum justum*, an active form of peace. At the same time the heart of the modern crisis becomes clear—the loss of a common criterion of justice.

During the Middle Ages, after years of multifarious

feuding between families and towns, after an era of widespread arbitrary justice, a general peace broke out when the individual legal persons renounced their power. These worked out their relationships with each other within a commonly accepted law of the land (*Landrecht*) and transferred the protection of that law to central authorities—the "judiciary" and its various organs.[1] The result of this was a clear separation of two essentially different kinds of power: the state's organs of law have means of implementation that are accepted, within the framework of the peace thus created, as the force of law. They are no longer the "power" that for one person is the means by which he tries to safeguard his rights but for another is an act of injustice to be resisted. Instead they protect the rights of all. They constitute "legal power", something fundamentally different from the law-breaking power of violence. Today a process is under way that may amount to the reversal of the medieval renunciation of power. The reversal could have various causes. Perhaps the state has ceased to defend justice and is palming off arbitrary whim in the guise of justice. On the other hand, it may be that ideological groups are creating their own partial ideas of justice, thereby breaking away from the universality of justice, in order to achieve their own

[1] Cf. H. Maier, *Worauf Frieden beruht* (Freiburg, 1981), 20ff.; U. Duchrow, *Christenheit und Weltverantwortung* (Stuttgart, 1970), 533ff.

ends. What underlies both is an ethical and religious revolution. On the question of what is right and wrong, consensus has collapsed.

We have just said that the reversal of the renunciation of power may be the fault of the state when it passes off injustice as law. Or it may be caused by the law-breaking partiality of a group bent on making its own rights the only law, which means that it too legitimizes injustice. Depending on which of the two it is, people will talk of a liberation movement or of terrorism. Of course, every form of terrorism will present itself as a liberation movement, and when there is no clear criterion of justice, it can do that very easily.

It is worth remembering that, in the first phase of German terrorism, when the phenomenon had hardly affected other Western countries, there was a widespread tendency in the West to regard the terrorists as true freedom-fighters, victims of a newly emerging state of totalitarianism. Only when the phenomenon became international and people had the chance to see the "freedom struggle" at close quarters did it become indisputably clear that here was a brutal violence, contemptuous of humanity, and that its idealized, anarchic freedom was conceived chiefly as a freedom to be violent and a freedom from law. On the other hand, people in Europe are always enthusiastically ready to celebrate every kind of terrorism in the Third World as a liberation movement. For more than twenty years Helmut Kuhn has been sharp-sightedly explaining the reason for this:

> As order divorced from justice becomes terrible, so unjust prosperity, obtained by exploitation and the suffering of others, becomes offensive. This is the reason for the bad conscience that spoils the Western world's enjoyment of its post-war prosperity and finds no solace in the thought of giving foreign aid.[2]

What is more, though the initial phase of European terrorism may be credited, despite everything, with a certain idealism, at least an idea of something, today the disintegration of justice, and with it the unleashing of violence, is proceeding apace. The world-wide network of drug-trafficking, coupled with prostitution, the arms traffic and the old criminal syndicates, is gradually becoming a threat to humanity. The loss of justice, without a great open war, is destroying peace from the inside and more effectively than the classic wars were ever able to do. It may be that, from an unexpected quarter and in an unusual form, something of the dimensions of a world war is developing.

The fourth way in which peace is destroyed has already been hinted at above; in fact, it is closely connected with what we have just said. It can happen that a state falls into the hands of groups that

[2] H. Kuhn, *Der Staat: Eine philosophische Darstellung* (Munich, 1967), 193.

palm off injustice as justice, destroying justice from
top to bottom, and thereby, in their own way, creating a peace that in reality is dictatorship. Such a
state, by the methods of modern mass-domination,
can produce total subjugation and so give an impression of order and tranquility, while people of uncompromising conscience are thrown into jail,
forced into exile or murdered. As Augustine asserted
emphatically, a state without justice is a great robber
band.[3] Hitler's *Reich* was such a robber state. Out-
wardly, it may look as if there is peace, but it is the
peace of the graveyard. The tragedy is that, under
total tyranny, there is no possibility at all of a war of
liberation. Dictatorship quietly sets itself up as the
triumph of peace. This is what the New Testament
means when it predicts that the Antichrist will
appear as the harbinger of "peace and security".[4]

---

[3] *De civitate Dei* IV, 4 (*Corpus Christianorum* XLVII, 101):
*Remota itaque iustitia quid sunt regna nisi magna latrocinia? quia et
latrocinia quid sunt nisi parva regna?*

[4] 1 Thessalonians 5:3 presents the rule of the slogan "peace
and security" as a sign of the imminent end of the world, but it
does not link it with the figure of the Antichrist. Later reflection
does make the connection, absolutely correctly in my opinion.
Soloviev does it in a very penetrating way in his story about the
Antichrist. Soloviev's Antichrist is the author of a book that has
aroused world-wide attention. Its title is "The Open Way to
Peace and Prosperity in the World". In the manifesto that he
issues after his proclamation as world ruler, he says: "Peoples of
the world! The promises have been fulfilled! World peace is

Here we confront the paradoxical aspect of our subject. What poses as definitive peace may well be the total destruction of peace.

2. The Foundation and Form of Justice

The heart of our contemporary problems can be seen in the third aspect of the crisis. Here again it becomes clear how closely connected religion is with peace and justice. We have shown that today peace is breaking up *within* nations, that agreement about what is right and wrong has collapsed. Now, what holds a society together and gives it peace is law. The fact that peace between nations has constantly been wrecked by war is connected with the lack of an effective international law, a law that not only orders a society on the inside but is also commonly recognized among the nations as their binding norm; they submit to it, whether or not it be to their advantage. Now if law ceases to have a commonly accepted content, it becomes powerless, and the distinction between legal power and wrongful power is blurred. The representatives of legal power become "pigs", and the representatives of wrongful power the cham-

---

ensured forever. . . ." Also important is the penetrating interpretation of the Antichrist traditions in J. Pieper, *Über das Ende der Zeit: Eine geschichtsphilosophische Betrachtung* (Munich, 1980), 113–36.

pions of liberty. Law without proof of identity looks like arbitrary whim, and all that is left is power: *Homo homini lupus*.

And so the question of peace is in practice identical with the question of law, and the real question for the survival of the human race is, therefore, the question of what constitutes the foundations and unalterable content of law. But where and how can an answer be found to the question? Or rather let us put it the other way round: Why has the distinction between right and wrong ceased to be obvious to us? Why can we not differentiate them? These questions require us to consider the foundation and fashioning of law in the modern world. Of course, once again this cannot take the form of a historical analysis. Instead, I shall try to focus on a few decisive points. As far as I can see, there are three.

a. *Authoritas—Utilitas*

First, there are the famous words of Thomas Hobbes: *Authoritas, non veritas facit legem*.[5] The Socratic question about what right and wrong really are, in themselves and according to the inner truth of things, independently of all traditions and enactments of law,

[5] M. Mettner, "Friede", in P. Eicher (ed.), *Neues Handbuch theologischer Grundbegriffe* I (Munich, 1981), 404–31, here 421. Cf. on Hobbes, H. Maier, "Hobbes", in Maier-Rausch-Denzer, *Klassiker des politischen Denkens* I (Munich, 1969), 351–75.

is dismissed as impractical.[6] The law is not based on
the discernible reality of right and wrong but on the
authority of the person with the power to enact it. It
comes about through legislation, and in no other
way. Its inner protection is thus the power to push it
through, not the truth of being. This thesis enabled
various things to happen. First of all, it helped political rule to become independent of the various other
powers in medieval society. It was used to support
the claims of absolute monarchies. But it also became
the axiom of legal positivism, which has been able to
establish itself widely since the nineteenth century.
The consequences are far-reaching. Now one government can declare to be legal what its neighbor
makes illegal. At the same time, in the minds of a
large number of politicians today (in other words, the
legislative *authoritas*), this is modified to mean that
the law has to mirror, and to translate into norms,
the value judgments actually found in society. When
majority opinion becomes in this way the only real
source of law and the essential criterion of *authoritas*,
the paradox is not in any way diminished. The man
condemned today may see himself as the pioneer of
the law of tomorrow and so feel justified to use every
means at his disposal to usher in the future, of which

[6] Still important for what it says about the nature and permanent validity of the Socratic question, see R. Guardini, *Der Tod
des Sokrates* (Berlin, 1943, new impression Mainz-Paderborn,
1987). Cf. also Kuhn, 24ff.

he regards himself as the custodian. If truth is as inaccessible as is here supposed, then there is no distinction in reality between right and wrong, no distinction between rightful and wrongful power, but only the pressure of the momentarily stronger group, the supremacy of the majority.

This notion of law is matched by an idea of peace that one might sum up as follows: *Utilitas, non veritas facit pacem.* In similar fashion to Adam Smith, Immanuel Kant developed his doctrine of perpetual peace largely along these lines:

> The spirit of commerce sooner or later takes hold of every people, and it cannot exist side by side with war. And of all the powers (or means) at the disposal of the power of the state, financial power can probably be relied on most. Thus states find themselves compelled to promote the noble cause of peace. . . . And wherever in the world there is a threat of war breaking out, they will try to prevent it by mediation, just as if they had entered into a permanent league for this purpose.[7]

[7] *Zum ewigen Frieden.* The edition I consulted was that of the Wissenschaftliche Buchgesellschaft, volume 6 (Darmstadt, 1964), 226. [For an English translation, see H. Reiss (ed.), *Kant's Political Writings* (Cambridge, 1970), 114.] Cf. Kuhn, 351ff.; Mettner, 422. Obviously, this citation is not intended as a presentation or evaluation of the entire, much richer and more profound thought of this Königsberg philosopher on the subject of peace.

In other words, it is a question of making egotism, man's strongest and most reliable power and the source of his conflicts, into a real instrument of peace, because it is precisely egotism that makes peace seem more useful than war. Realistic politics will doubtless take account of this view and see it as an element in the peacemaking process. But on its own, as history since Kant adequately proves, it is insufficient for the building of perpetual peace.

b. Three Fundamental Rights—The Ambivalence of the Rights of Man Doctrine

The two ideas just mentioned (*authoritas* and *utilitas*) present themselves in our post-metaphysical age. In a situation in which the unknowability of the true and man's incapacity for the good seem to have become absolute certainties, the attempt is made to build justice and peace on the foundation of authority and utility. Opposed to these two post-metaphysical ideas, the political effects of which are obvious, is a more strongly metaphysical current of thought. I am thinking of the three fundamental rights laid down by John Locke in his *Second Treatise of Government* (1690): life, freedom, property. The background to this is the *Magna Carta,* the *Bill of Rights,* and ultimately the natural law tradition.[8] Here is a quite

[8] Important on this point and what follows is Kuhn, 262–66. See also E.-W. Böckenförde and R. Spaemann (eds.), *Menschen*

explicit claim that the rights of the person precede
the state's enactments of law. Locke's way of expressing the rights of man doctrine is clearly directed
against the state. It is of revolutionary significance.
Not surprisingly, long before Marx, the Enlightenment developed a revolutionary tradition of its own.
The old doctrine of the just war turned into the doctrine of a struggle for perpetual peace to be con-
ducted in the form of world-wide civil war.[9] This
gives an inkling of the ambivalence of the rights of
man doctrine. When the concept of freedom is
hypertrophied and the state is regarded essentially as
an enemy, peace does not have a chance. But there is
a sound core to the idea of human rights, and so it
continues to be a guide to the truth and a protective
barrier against positivism. There is something that is
right in itself, and this constitutes the true bond
among men, because it stems from our common
nature.

Attempting to uncover the roots of the crisis of
justice and peace shows us what can heal it. Law can
be the effective power of peace only when the yard-
stick for measuring it is not in our hands. The law is
molded, not created, by us. In other words, there can

rechte und Menschenwürde (Stuttgart, 1987), especially the contribution of G. Stourzh, "Die Begründung der Menschenrechte im
englischen und amerikanischen Verfassungsdenken des 17. und
18. Jahrhunderts", 78–90.
[9] Cf. Mettner, 422f.

be no foundation for law without transcendence. When God and the basic pattern of human existence laid down by him are ousted from public consciousness and relegated to the private, merely subjective realm, the concept of law dissolves into thin air and, with it, the foundation of peace.

3. WHAT THE CHURCH CAN AND MUST DO—WHAT SHE NEITHER CAN NOR SHOULD DO

This brings us to the third part of our discussion, the contribution that religion can and should make to peace. I have already indicated above why I am taking religion concretely to mean Church. I think it is necessary to distinguish between what the Church must do for peace and what she must not and cannot do.

a. The Tradition and Protection of the Basic Criterion

The Church's first task in this area is to keep alive, in fidelity to her holy tradition, the basic criterion of justice and to detach it from the arbitrariness of power. What her great founders have seen and said, what Jesus and his witnesses saw and said, the Church must carry through the years as a great light for the human race. In each generation, she must shine that light on present-day questions and offer the Word given to her as the answer to the problems of the age. She must carry conviction and help men to see with and through Jesus what they cannot see by their own powers. She must ensure that in the conflict between *utilitas* and *veritas*, between *authoritas* and *veritas*, truth does not founder. Man has been given an organ for apprehending truth as well as an organ for determining utility. There is nothing wrong with utility, but when it is made absolute, it becomes a force for evil. Utility destroys itself when it disregards truth. The same is true of *authoritas*. The trouble is that the organ of utility and the organ of power are more palpable and more immediate in their effects than the organ of truth. That is why the organ of truth needs assistance, needs support. This is what the Church's task ought to be: to give this otherwise all too easily suppressed faculty the strength it needs.

The task of the Church in this area is, therefore, first and foremost "education", taking that word in the great sense it had for the Greek philosophers. She must break open the prison of positivism and awaken man's receptivity to the truth, to God, and thus to the power of conscience. She must give men the courage to live according to conscience and so keep open the narrow pass between anarchy and tyranny, which is none other than the narrow way of peace. In society she must create the conviction that can support good law. For, though we just now rejected the idea of majority opinion as the source of law, it is also clear that law cannot be permanently effective unless it has some kind of public credibility. In this consideration, it must appear as a highly questionable development that the modern administration of justice has quite publicly ceased to regard moral and religious values as goods deserving of legal protection; it seems to think that only material goods and the libertarian freedom of the individual need defense. In this consideration, it must appear as a highly questionable development that the same holds true in the Church. Hardly anyone looks upon faith as a good deserving of protection, at least not when it is in conflict with individual freedom or public opinion.

b. The Renunciation of Direct Political Action

Alongside this primary task of creating conviction, forming conscience and fashioning community as a space for peace is the mission of the Church's office-bearers, supported by the conviction of the faithful, to speak out publicly on questions of the moment and to be advocates of peace. In our own times this has been taken up with great passion. In addition to the classical channels of communication in the Church, many kinds of commissions and institutions are developing that dedicate themselves passionately to the question of peace and try to come up with the right words in reply. Not everything that comes to light by this means is enlightened. But the concern itself is, without doubt, a proper part of one of the Church's real tasks. What the Church has to remember is that, though the sources of law have been entrusted to her safekeeping, she does not have any specific answers to concrete political questions. She must not make herself out to be the sole possessor of political reason. She points out paths for reason to follow, and yet reason's own responsibilities remain.

All this comes together in the Church's most interior and yet also most human task: the task of making, not just talking about, peace, in deeds of love. No social service of the state can replace Christian love in both its spontaneous and organized forms. In fact, social service totally disintegrates when it loses the inspiration of the love that comes from faith. The Church's fidelity to her true nature is shown in her ability to support human beings in the vocation to love, to bring the vocation of love to maturity and to give it concrete form in the life of the community. Through the power of love, the Church must serve the poor, the sick, the lost, the oppressed. She must go into prison, into the suffering of mind and body, as far as the dark way of death. In areas torn by the strife the human race always has experienced and always will experience, the Church must give men the strength to survive and, with the power of forgiveness, awaken the capacity to make a new start. Only

the man who can forgive can build and preserve
peace.[10]

All this goes to show the limits of the Church's
task and powers. She cannot enforce peace. She could
not do it in the past, and she cannot do it in the
future. She must not be transformed into a kind of
political peace movement, whose only *raison d'être*
would be the attaining of perpetual world peace. The
planned "peace council" of religions is, therefore,
because of the nature of the Church, an impossibility.
The leaders of the Church have no authority to take
direct political action. They have not received a man-
date for it from the faithful, certainly not from the
Lord himself. In fact, one ought rather to say that the
attempt to bring about a world-wide empire of peace
through a world-wide union of religions is perilously
close to the third temptation of Jesus: "All the kingdoms of the world I will give you, if you fall down
and worship me" (cf. Mt 4:9).[11] In this way of thinking, world peace almost inevitably becomes the *Sum-*

---

[10] On the connection between peace and forgiveness, see H.
Schlier, "Der Friede nach dem Apostel Paulus", in his *Der Geist
und die Kirche* (Frieburg, 1980), 117–33, especially 133.

[11] Pieper, 123, quotes in a similar context the statement: "A
world organization might be what ushers in that most deadly and
invincible of all tyrannies, the final reign of the Antichrist." "The
drawback of a world state embodying the Kantian ideal of there
being no more real 'external wars' is that in place of war there
would be police operations which would take the form of pest
control" (124). Cf. Kuhn, 355: "It is as martyr that the Church is

mum bonum, to which everyone submits and for whose attainment all other religious acts and values are mere means. But a God who becomes the means to supposedly higher ends is no longer God; in fact, he has given away his divinity to something higher, whose cause he must serve. It is obvious that peace established in this way is, of its very nature, in danger of turning into either the totalitarianism that allows only one way of thinking or world-wide civil war.

c. Witness and Ministry of Love

Consequently, the Church does less, not more, for peace if she abandons her own sphere of faith, education, witness, counsel, prayer, and serving love and changes into an organization for direct political action. In so doing, she blocks access to the wellsprings from which the powers of peace and reconciliation continually flow. Precisely because the utmost must be done for peace, the Church must remain true to her real nature. Only when she respects her limits is she limitless, and only then can her ministry of love and witness become a call to all men. What the Church ultimately has to contribute to peace has been persuasively summed up, I think, in some words of Metropolitan Damaskinos. I endorse them without

---

most truly herself. But as an organization for creating fraternity among men she founders on the earthly supremacy of politics."

qualification and so would like to conclude by quoting them:

> It is my considered opinion that, over and above her social service, the contribution of the Orthodox Church to peace, freedom, justice, and brotherhood among the nations consists in a witness of love. . . . The Church's role cannot be identified with any kind of political strategy or with the political expediency of the authorities of governments among which her peoples live. In this context the Orthodox Churches' scope for initiative and action is restricted. Her witness and presence bring with them dangers which may lead her leaders to martyrdom. . . . But it is precisely this love that is ready for martyrdom which ultimately strengthens the will of the Orthodox Churches. It enables them, in collaboration with their brethren in the other Christian Churches and confessions, to bear witness—the witness of faith and love—in a world that perhaps has more need of it than ever.[12]

[12] Metropolitan Damaskinos Papandreous, "Contribution de l'Église orthodoxe à la réalisation des idéaux chrétiens de paix, de liberté, de fraternité et d'amour entre les peuples, et la suppression des discriminations raciales", in *Weisheit Gottes—Weisheit der Welt*, Festschrift für J. Ratzinger, 2 (St. Ottilien, 1987), 1333–43, here 1342f.

III

Faith and Social Responsibility

Prefatory Note: The award of the great Leopold Kunschak Prize, which was bestowed on me, to my
surprise and joy, on March 9, 1991, gave me the
opportunity to give an account of my own relationship to the questions of Catholic social doctrine and
at the same time to attempt a statement of principle
about the connection between faith and social
responsibility. My own theological starting point was
indeed obviously far removed from the questions
posed here; but it has become clearer to me, in retro-
spect, that this distance was only apparent.

1. The Basis of Faith
and the Social Relevance of Faith

When I began my theological studies, just after the
end of the Second World War, the decisive motivating factor for me was the question of the *ratio spei*,
the question of the reason for our hope, as the First

Letter of Peter puts it (3:15), in a phrase that was rightly understood in the Middle Ages as the basis for all theology. According to the Apostle, we must bear in ourself the reason for our hope in such a way that this *logos* can become *apologia*: the word of hope wishes to become the answer to the question of the man who seeks to discover where hope is and who wishes to understand the reason why one is permitted to hope. This New Testament phrase, heavy with substance, is a description of the essential process of all theology, but it applies in a particular manner to that section of the theological endeavor which desires to investigate the basis, the foundation of faith and its hope, wishing to give an account of faith—a discipline that was first called apologetics (from *apologia*, the Greek word for "answer") and then also fundamental theology (because it asks the question about the foundation).

The reason for our faith and the communicability of its hope and of the meaning it gives to our life: these were the questions I wished above all to address when I began my studies, and this is why I decided to specialize in the area of fundamental theology. The question thus posed goes to the root of faith. But it is not in the least divorced from the world. For the chief objection to Christianity appeared to me to be its apparent failure to transform the world and man. In the twentieth century after Christ, national socialism and communism had come to power.

While the testimony they gave against the Redeemer of the world did not appear to me for one moment to be convincing, let alone alluring, in its negative way it did put faith to a harsh test: It was obvious that the world had not become better in twenty centuries of Christian proclamation, for the horrors that were now taking place were at least the equal of those that had occurred in pre-Christian times. Was it still really possible to call the years after Christ "years of salvation"? Were not the years on which we looked back terrible years of "un-salvation", and must we not indeed expect perhaps even worse years in the future?

Forty years later, I found the questions that had moved me at that period formulated with utter clarity by Julien Green, although, naturally, the answer he gives is one I cannot share. At the end of his book on Saint Francis, this great author writes:

> World War II shook my soul the way one shakes somebody by the shoulders. . . . The world at war struck me as one vast atrocity. My mind gradually came to the conclusion that the Gospel was a failure. Christ himself had wondered about the faith he would find on earth at his second coming. The souls he had touched and drawn to him seemed isolated in the storm unleased by madmen. Almost at the midpoint between the first Christmas and the hell humanity was writhing in, a man had appeared on earth, another Christ, the Francis of my childhood,

but he had failed. Failed? Apparently. . . . He was convinced that salvation would come through the Gospel. The Gospel was eternity, the Gospel had only just begun. What were twenty centuries in the eyes of God?[1]

2. THE TWO PATHS TAKEN BY THEOLOGY
AFTER THE SECOND WORLD WAR

a. Faith as Desecularization

I have never believed for one moment that the *apologia* of the Gospel could consist in pointing to the effect it would have at some future time. On the contrary, one would truly have to concede the validity of Karl Marx's objection that the Gospel has had time enough to prove its possibilities. But the question of what kind of promise the Gospel has for this history of ours, what it promises us and what it does not—this question was and remains unavoidable: it had to stand at the center of an "*apologia* of hope". In this way, the problem of the social responsibility of faith belongs to the center of fundamental theology's task. It is, of course, true that this problem was curiously defused in the theological context of the period just after the War. The political Catholicism of the

[1] J. Green, *Frère François*, English trans.: *God's Fool: The Life and Times of Francis of Assisi* (San Francisco, 1985), 273.

period between the World Wars had collapsed with the appearance of the Third Reich, and it was not possible for it to return. The spirit of the Youth Movement nourished skepticism against all kinds of groups and organizations. After faith was forcibly deprived of all political responsibility in 1933, it had received new power and depth precisely by being compelled to find a purely religious form. The loss of power had been an advantage for it. It had become purer. Its own hope, for which there is no substitute, had emerged in its indestructible greatness precisely in the places of earthly hopelessness, in the grayness of the concentration camps and in the courts of those who held power. Thus, there was a desire to avoid every new amalgamation of faith with the political level. The desire for a purely religious realization of the Gospel determined the direction of theology, while of course—as we shall soon see—there was certainly a vigilant awareness in the political sphere of the secular responsibility of faith.

The confrontation between Romano Guardini and Carl Sonnenschein in the Berlin of the 1920s seems to me characteristic of the experience people had had in those years, the experience that now indicated the path ahead. In his memoirs, Guardini gives this description of Sonnenschein's position:

> Sonnenschein had stood deep in the modernist movement. When the crisis came for him, he had not only separated himself from this movement: he

must also have dismissed theological problems as a whole. His standpoint in Berlin was: "We are in a besieged city in which there are no problems but only slogans." This formula may be impressive, but it is false. . . . Genuine praxis . . . that is, correct conduct, comes from the truth. And one must struggle to find the truth.[2]

Guardini goes on to formulate his own position, which is thereby outlined in its essence:

As time passed, I became less and less concerned . . . with immediate effect. What I had wanted from the outset, first instinctively and then more and more consciously, was to bring the truth to light. Truth is a power, but only when one does not demand that it have any immediate effect.[3]

These sentences of this great teacher seem to be a completely appropriate indication of the true essence of a new distinction between the secular order and faith, as well as the essence of a correct praxeology, a correct statement of the relationship between faith and praxis. But the positions taken in the period shortly after the War moved on and at first scarcely developed at all the tendency to take concrete responsibility for the world that is undeniably contained in Guardini's position (as the further development of his thought showed). The new slo-

[2] R. Guardini, *Bericht über mein Leben: Autobiographische Aufzeichnungen* (Düsseldorf, 1984), 111.

[3] Ibid., 109.

gan was supplied by Bultmann, who attempted here to adopt Heidegger as an instrument for the interpretation of biblical revelation: this slogan was "desecularization". A strangely dualistic position, which continues to have its effect today, developed from this program: the Christian faith, which itself is interpreted as desecularization, aims, not at the sanctification of the world, but at its secularization. It is the release of the world into its secular character, an intentional desacralization. The inherent line of development of Christianity itself is realized precisely in the increasing emancipation of the world from the religious dimension. Thus there would be no greater error than the desire to create a Christian society. The more radically secular the world becomes, the better it is. Christian action in the world could not consist of communicating to society Christian patterns of order: It is seen, on the contrary, in the renunciation of such confusions between faith and world. We can find one of the most recent examples of the continued effect of such positions in the book *Le Rêve de Compostelle*, in which a group of French theologians reacts to the youth meeting at Santiago de Compostela by accusing the Pope of a backward-looking romanticism that aims at a reestablishing of Christendom: one ought to want the opposite of this.[4] In this conception, desecularization and secular-

[4] R. Luneau and P. Ladrière (eds.), *Le Rêve de Compostelle. Vers la restauration d'une Europe chrétienne?* (Paris: Centurion, 1989).

ization go hand in hand and produce strange paradoxes. It is precisely representatives of the purely religious path who tend to become actively involved in Marxist parties, clearly in order to push Christianity aside into pure unworldliness. Paradoxically, this political neutrality turned into a new form of political activity.

Of course in those early days after the War, one could as yet scarcely foresee these dialectical leaps of a new turning to the religious center. On the contrary, this was the great hour of Christian politicians, after the collapse of the anti-Christian madness. The new construction was based very consciously on the ethical principles of Christianity, and thus there was a conscious linkage to the spiritual center of faith itself, while there was independence from ecclesiastical directives, in the appropriate autonomy of the state. The social responsibility of faith was the decisive directive to the conscience of a generation of politicians whom we can but name with gratitude as the fathers of a new Europe: Adenauer, Schuman, de Gasperi, de Gaulle, but also men such as Raab, Figl and Kunschak.

b. Faith as Politics

The concept of the secular world, which I should wish to call a Manichaean error, was bound sooner or later to call forth an opposite effect, which emerged as early as the 1960s, first in the form of political theology and then in the shape of liberation theology with its many variants. The phenomenon is so well known that I need not give any further description of it. One brief reference to a central concept must suffice. Exegesis had long noted that the "Kingdom of God" was the central concept of Jesus' proclamation. In the radical-eschatological interpretation of the figure of Jesus, which began with Albert Schweitzer and was then deepened philosophically and theologically by Bultmann, this meant that Jesus had nothing to say that was inner-worldly: he pointed only to that which was "wholly other". The program of desecularization and seculari-zation corresponded to this view. But now, in the face of growing social distress and inescapable Chris-tian responsibility, this interpretation changed into its own opposite. Today, the "kingdom" is the central slogan of all the forms of liberation theology. It is characteristic that one now speaks simply of the "kingdom"—without mentioning God—and that this is understood now as the ideal human society. It is the aim of faith and the task of all theology to work to bring about the "kingdom". The central word of faith becomes a political concept, an expres-sion of the goal of all good politics. Faith itself thereby becomes political ideology. Politics has absorbed faith into itself.

3. The Social Responsibility of Faith

Between these two extremes, which have in many cases united to form a strange alliance, there stands today the question of the social and political responsibility of faith. In this constellation, this question has in fact become the central point of all fundamental theology's endeavors; what is at stake here is nothing more and nothing less than the question of whether we as believers are permitted to hope and what the genuine contents of our faith are. In the final section of my reflections, I should like to sketch only briefly the outline of an answer.

Here, I shall tackle the question of the social responsibility of faith paradigmatically on the basis of a text from the Old Testament that became a central christological text in the New Testament and teaches us to understand the unity of the Testaments correctly. It seems to me that the correct understanding of our problem, indeed the appropriate understanding of the Christian faith as a whole, depends on the correct understanding of the relationship between Old and New Testaments. The opposing positions I have attempted to sketch in my historical review are based on a misunderstanding of this relationship. Harnack, who categorized Christ's message as strictly individualistic and thereby reduced it to an "ethics of attitude" in the sense of Max Weber, had demanded that Marcion's legacy finally be executed and the New Testament separated from the Old. Bultmann's position of desecularization is based on the same hermeneutical starting point. Bultmann, too, is unable to recognize any unity between the Testaments; for him, the only way in which the Old Testament leads over into the New is through its failure. A New Testament torn away from the Old Testament is necessarily without a world; a Jesus torn away from the life context of the Old Testament is merely a moralist who can inspire attitudes; the "salvation of the world" does not stand within his horizon.

In the case of the radicalized political theologians, on the other hand, the relationship between Old and New Testaments is just the reverse: the New Testament is taken back into the Old; redemption becomes the Exodus, interpreted in a political way, as the secular act of liberation, and thus the Kingdom of God becomes the product of the human act of liberation. In this process, it is not only Christology that totally loses its own features; the Old Testament itself is deprived of its dynamic that points ahead and upward, and it is turned around even in its own direction of movement.

But let us look at a text that will demonstrate this in an exemplary manner: the first of the Servant Songs, Isaiah 42:1–4 (5–9). We are told here three times in four verses that the Servant, the one whom God has chosen, brings "justice" to the peoples,

establishes it on earth, genuinely gives justice. The
Hebrew word *mishpat*, translated here as "justice", is
one of the more commonly used words of the Old
Testament, appearing no less than 425 times in the
Hebrew Bible.[5] The nuances of its meaning can be
extremely variable in individual cases, but all move
within the sphere of justice, righteousness, law, judgment, so that P. Uys can define *mishpat* simply as
"the God-given norm to ensure a well-ordered society".[6] The fact that it is set in parallelism three times
to *sedaqah*, "righteousness", points in the same direction. It seems, therefore, that the task of the Servant
of the Lord, this mysterious messianic figure, is to
give justice to the world. It is not surprising that liberation theology's interpretation of Scripture has
believed it could use this to build a bridge between
Marx and the Bible, since here the *mishpat* of the
poor, the action to establish right order, appears as
the central messianic task.[7]

We must therefore look a little more closely, in
order to understand what we learn in this text about
the figure of Christ and about the hope that has its
origin in him and about the commission he gives.

[5] Cf. B. Johnson, "Mishpat", in Botterweck, Ringgren and
Fabry (eds.), *Theol. Wörterbuch zum Alten Testament*, 5:93–107,
particularly 95.

[6] Quoted by Johnson, 101.

[7] J. Merendino, *Marx and the Bible* (New York, 1974), esp.
109ff.

The as yet unknown Servant stands in a clear parallel to the figure of Moses, indeed precisely as the fulfillment of the promise: "The Lord your God will raise up from your midst, among your brothers, a prophet like me. You are to listen to him. . . . I will put my words in his mouth, and he will tell them all that I charge him to say" (Dt 18:15, 18).[8] In the Old Testament tradition, the decisive action in Moses' activity as mediator is not the act of leading the people out of Egypt but the act of handing on the Law at Mount Sinai. It is only through this that the Exodus from the foreign land takes on meaning and stability. For the people is set free and becomes a free nation of its own only by becoming a legal community. Lack of freedom is the condition of being without law. This is why the gift of the Law is the real establishment of liberation—and of a Law that is truly justice, namely, right order in relationship to one another, in relationship to creation and in relationship to the Creator. Man's freedom can exist only in the correct mutual allocation of these freedoms, and this is possible only if they all take the freedom of God and his truth as their criterion. True justice, just justice can come into existence only when the true God is recognized aright, so that man, too, recognizes himself aright and orders his exis-

[8] For the parallel to Moses, cf. the exemplary exposition by C. Westermann, *Das Buch Jesaja. Kap. 40–66,* ATD 19 (Göttingen, 1966), 77–81.

tence in a life with others on the basis of God. This is
why Sinai was for Israel the criterion and the foundation of its freedom; it always lost its freedom to the
extent that it departed from justice, returning to a
condition without law and thereby falling back into
servitude.[9]

At this point, we must pause for a moment. If one
identifies liberation with the victorious Exodus, one
looks on it as an event of power whose success, as it
were, automatically transposes the individual and the
entire people into the condition of freedom. But if
one recognizes that the essence of the liberation lies
in the gift of the Law bestowed by God, then one
sees that liberation is always linked to freedom and
can be communicated only through freedom. More
precisely, it is linked to a double mediation: the
mediation through reason that opens itself, that
makes itself accessible to God and thus becomes able
to discern justice and injustice; and it is linked to the
mediation through will that puts into action what has
been recognized. Since man in his historical existence always retains the freedom to refuse these
mediations, freedom never attains complete perfec-
tion within history.

This permits us now to understand the figure of
the new Moses whom the prophet describes under
the title "Servant of the Lord". Unlike the first

[9] I have set out these connections in greater detail in my book
Kirche, Ökumene und Politik (Einsiedeln, 1987), 235ff.

Moses, he no longer merely communicates justice to
Israel alone but "bears it out to the peoples" (Is 42:1)
and establishes it on earth (42:4). The previously iso-
lated individual event becomes universal; salvation
now is for the whole world, which is gathered
together and reconciled in the common justice of the
one God. But this does not take place by means of
conquest and subjection. The prophet says that the
Servant of God "does not cry out" in order to distinguish him from the type of "liberators" who declare
the establishment of their own power to be liberation
and redemption. A trait that had already been increasingly emphasized by tradition in the figure of
Moses now emerges with complete clarity in the Servant of God: he suffers for justice. He does not meet
injustice with new injustice: he endures injustice in
suffering and thereby sets limits to it; he transforms it
from within. If one adds up all these elements, it
becomes clear that Law and prophets flow together
in the figure of the Servant of God to form a new
unity: the Servant does what Moses did. He gives
mishpat, he gives the justice that comes from God and
thereby brings about the reconciliation of freedoms,
which is the only true form of human freedom. But
this justice is now no longer Torah but precisely
mishpat; it is no longer a firmly defined national body
of laws but an open form of law that must attain ever
anew the synthesis of universality and particularity, so
that it remains open to future history and its chal-

lenges, while yet opposing every arbitrariness with the immovable criterion of the truth.

The Servant of the Lord in Isaiah remains expectation; he takes up the promise of the "other prophet" from Deuteronomy 18 and develops it. Those who encountered Jesus could not avoid seeing in him the fulfillment of this hope. Thus the introductory words from the Song of the Servant (Is 42:1) stand over his Baptism—like a title set over the entire activity of Jesus that explains in advance who and what he is (Mk 1:11). Jesus' claim on the Old Testament is clearly presented precisely through this connection and also the extent of its substance specified. In him, Law and prophets now truly flow together in the way we have just suggested. But this implies that any reduction of his message to an ethics of attitude, and any individualistic or existentialistic interpretation in the sense of the ideology of desecularization, misses the essence of his figure. It also means that a political interpretation of Jesus that makes him a failed rebel paints a totally false picture of him. Jesus was not Barabbas or Spartacus, but precisely Jesus. He possesses the entire concreteness of all the social and legal directives of the prophets and also, therefore, the entire Law, as this is illuminated and universalized by the prophets. Faith in him goes beyond the social and political realm, but, precisely in this, it is a faith in social responsibility. The social dimension is included in faith—not in the form of a ready-made

party program or a ready-made order for the structure of the world. It is contained in faith precisely in
the mode of responsibility, and this means that it
requires mediation through reason and will. Reason
and will must attempt to make concrete and to put
into practice the criterion of God's *mishpat*, set up by
faith, in changing historical situations, always in the
essential imperfectibility of man's action within history. It is not permitted to man to set up the "Kingdom", but he is charged to go toward the Kingdom
through justice and love. The necessary mediation
contained in the concept of *mishpat* indicates at the
same time the precisely theological and methodological *locus* of Catholic (Christian) social doctrine.
Faith's hope always goes infinitely farther than all our
realizations, reaching into the realm of the eternal;
but precisely the fact that this hope is given to us
gives us the courage to take up again and again,
despite all inadequacy, the struggle for a just order
that is the form of freedom and builds up a dam
against the tyranny of injustice.

PART TWO

ASSESSMENT AND FORECAST

I

PATHS OF FAITH IN THE REVOLUTIONARY CHANGE OF THE PRESENT DAY*

The year 1989 led to dramatic revolutions in the political and intellectual landscape of Europe that no one could have predicted even a short time before. The new element in this revolution was the fact that it did not come about through political or military violence but through new departures and revolutionary changes in the intellectual order, which simply removed the basis from the old structures of power and led to their collapse almost overnight. Thus this process not only affects states that were previously dominated by the Marxist ideology but has a world-wide significance as well. It goes beyond the political

* The first version of this text was delivered on December 16, 1989, at Rieti while the impression of the events in Eastern Europe was still fresh, as an attempt at a first reflection on the causes and consequences of what had happened; the version presented here was given as a lecture on February 15, 1990, at the Sapienza University in Rome. On the occasion of the celebration of the 1400th anniversary of the Council of Toledo, on February 24, 1990, in Madrid, I gave this lecture in a form altered in keeping with the occasion.

field, particularly since it came from the metapolitical sphere itself and then of course brought to light the political force of originally nonpolitical factors. It would also, therefore, be inappropriate to harbor cheap feelings of satisfaction about the failure of others; rather, we are all called to reflect on the intellectual foundations on which paths into the future can be built, and on the foundations on which they cannot. Consequently, the reflections that follow, while linked to the political events of the year 1989, are directed to the metapolitical dimension that has appeared in all its urgency in these events.

1. THE CRISIS OF MARXISM AS A QUESTION PUT TO THE WESTERN WORLD

a. The Metapolitical Foundations of the Political-Economic Crisis

We shall begin our examination with the facts, in order to discern their inner motivating forces and thus to find criteria for the future. The first question we must pose is: What was it really that collapsed in the course of the years 1989 and 1990? To begin with, one can and must say simply that Marxism failed as an all-embracing interpretation of reality and as a directive for action in history. Its promise of freedom, equality and welfare for all was not verified by the empirical facts; it was shown to be false on the basis of political and economic facts. Although these assessments are correct, one would remain on a superficial level if one were to be content with them. Rather, we must take one step farther and ask: But what is specifically false in this interpretation of the world and in the praxis deduced from it? An exact observation of the events leads directly to the heart of the matter: the power of the spirit, the power of convictions, of suffering and of hopes, has thrown down the existing structures. This means that the materialism which wanted to reduce the spirit to a mere consequence of material structures, to the mere superstructure of the economic system, has been brought down. But here we are no longer speaking only of the problem of Marxism and its world of states—we are speaking about ourselves. For materialism is a problem that affects us all; its breakdown compels all of us to an examination of conscience.

This is why it is necessary to pause somewhat at this point and to ask what is the real core of a materialistic ideology. It does not consist in the total denial of spirit: materialism, too, admits that spirit has appeared on the scene at some place or other in history and that it must be distinguished from the merely material from then on. The essence of modern materialism is more subtle: it consists in the way in which the relationship between matter and spirit is conceived. Here, matter is the first and original element; it is matter, not the Logos, that stands at the beginning. Everything develops out of matter in a process of contingencies that becomes the process of necessities. Spirit is never more than the product of matter. If one knows the laws of matter and can manipulate these, then one can also direct the course of the spirit. One changes the spirit by rearranging its material conditions. Thus one can enlarge and remodel history in a mechanical way by enlarging and remodeling structures.[1]

[1] Naturally, it would be necessary to elaborate in greater detail and precision this fundamental diagnosis of the essence of modern materialism in general, in view of dialectical and historical materialism in particular. This was not possible in the limited space of this lecture. The specific character of this type of materialism comes first and foremost from the introduction of the factor of work into the materialistic way of looking at reality. But the fundamental presupposition remains the thesis of the primacy of matter vis-à-vis consciousness, which is broadened but not abolished through a dialectical view of the relationship between nature and consciousness. Through work—this is the thesis— man has an effect on nature, changing it in its turn, and the development of consciousness takes place in this confrontation. Dialectical materialism intends thereby to outgrow a merely mechanical materialism; it claims "to posit in the place of a mechanistic (or even pantheistic) way of looking at nature and man a thoroughgoing materialistic doctrine of the development of man which embraces all the spheres of reality and at the same time takes into account their specific particularities". This is how the *Philosophische Wörterbuch*, edited by G. Klaus and M. Buhr in the Bibliographical Institute in Leipzig, 2d ed. (1965), 329a, characterizes the claim to novelty and definitiveness of the type of

This materialistic arrogance has been proved to be an error. It is true that the spirit does depend to a good extent on its material conditions, but it transcends these. One cannot free man from his freedom by lining with concrete the channels along which it must move. The presumption that claims one can construct the perfect man and the perfect society with structural formulas is the real core of modern materialism, and this core has been shown to be an error.

---

materialism established by Mark and Engels. It is along this path that the integration of history and society into a scientifically transparent and governable regularity is to be totally attained—a goal that the more "contemplative" or "metaphysical" orientations of earlier forms of materialism had not been able to reach. Accordingly, the Lexicon continues (329a–b): "Thus it became possible for the first time in the history of human thought to apply materialism in the explanation of societal life and to uncover the material motivating forces and the laws of societal life: thus for the first time a scientific theory of society was established." It is precisely this claim of "being scientific" that has failed in recent events, in the course of which a freedom that abolishes the "laws of societal development" emerged in opposition to these "laws". In this Lexicon, the two articles "Materialismus" (325–30) and "Materialismus, dialektischer und historischer" (330–40), as well as the one on matter (341–44), still deserve to be read, as semi-official presentations of Marxist philosophy. Much information and a rich bibliography: W. Nieke, "Materialismus", in J. Ritter and K. Gründer (eds.), *Historisches Wörterbuch der Philosophie* 5 (Basel and Stuttgart, 1980), 843–50; W. Knispel, W. Goerdt and H. Dahm, "Materialismus, dialektischer", ibid., 851–59.

To count on the mechanical instead of on the spiritual, the eternal, is to miscalculate in the long run.

If this is correct, then one particular type of belief in science is also thereby called immediately into question; this belief in turn is something that goes far beyond the domain of Marxist power. Science in the narrower sense of the term refers to the realm of the necessary, which can be reduced to strict rules and leads in this way to objectively verifiable certainty. But this means that science, so understood, cannot deal with the realm of what is free, that is, with the genuinely human dimension of man and his social bonds. However, the fascination exercised by an all-embracing concept of science, a concept able to deal with man no less precisely than with the things of physics, has led to the transgression of this boundary. From as early as the time of Auguste Comte, all effort has gone into gaining a complete knowledge of man as a being governed by rules, to filling in all the blank spaces in the map of the scientific world. The result is the emergence, in all its variations, of the fundamental concept of social science, which appears in the East as Marxist sociology and in the West as positivist sociology. In both cases this sociology proposes the "project of modernity" (to use Jürgen Habermas' term).[2]

[2] I take the references to Habermas from the important essay by R. Hofmann, "Soziologie als theologische Grunddisziplin? Zur vergessenen Metaphysik der Sozialwissenschaften", in *Internat. kath. Zeitschrift* 19 (1990), 453–66, particularly 456.

There is no space here to explain more thoroughly the common methodological fundamental starting point of this kind of human science, which lies behind all the differences between Marxism and positivism; this human science regards itself as the new metaphysics, as the interpretation of the bases of human existence. Let it suffice to refer once again to Habermas, for whom personal existence is not to be seen as an independent variable but as "an essential dimension of the species, which realizes itself (first of all) in a historical process within one wholly specific time and society". The concept of person now denotes "an individual which has come into being in and through socialization and cannot at all be conceived of independently of society. This individual is produced or made, so to speak, in the mechanism of socialization."[3] The attempt to treat man "scientifically" in the narrowest sense of this word includes the determinism that comes from the antecedent materialism. An idea of science that is formed on the basis of what is not free is transposed to the realm of what is free, namely, the human realm, in order to make possible a "physics of man" in which there exist necessary laws and exact predictions.[4] If this theory is

---

[3] This is how B. Hamann, *Sozialisationstheorie auf dem Prüfstand* (Bad Hellbrunn, 1981), 46, characterizes the position of Habermas; cf. R. Hofmann, 461.

[4] M. Kriele, *Befreiung und politische Aufklärung* (Freiburg, 1980), 78–82, has enlightening observations on this area of questions.

taken consistently, it demands by its very nature the exclusion of the factor of freedom. The Marxist system merely translated these fundamental presuppositions with all stringency into political action: the suppression of freedom by the system is not an abuse of thought but rather its logical application. This is why the outbreak of freedom in practice against the system on the streets of the Eastern European capitals has far-reaching theoretical consequences too. Not only does it call Marxist thinking into question: it is equally a question posed to our way of basing human science on methodological foundations that exclude the *humanum*. Thus what has happened here in the political sphere is a real contribution to the fundamental question of what freedom is, and of what man is.

A third aspect of these events seems clear to me. What has happened has also called into question one particular form of the idea of progress. The word "progress" has become a satellite of the post-Hegelian philosophy of history. It presupposes the mechanistic interpretation of history we have just criticized. "Progress" can be employed here as a party label that sells well. In the socialist camp, progress was regarded quite simply as whatever served the construction of socialism. But there is also a superficial liberalism that is no less partisan. Freedom is equated with the absence of ties, and everything that removes ties appears to be progress. And ultimately, there exists the "technologistic" variant of the belief in progress, which sees man's progress in the growth of technical ability as such. Romano Guardini spoke in this connection of the "idiocy of the belief in progress".[5] Wherever progress is seen as a necessary process of the legitimate development of history, it is located below the level of what is genuinely human and in its depths it is conceived against man. Personal freedom and ethical responsibility for oneself can then be seen only as factors that interfere with such legitimacy. The massive appearance of this "interference factor" in recent years is an event that gives hope—and is at the same time a fact that compels us to reflect and to change our way of thinking.

Here, of course, we cannot avoid the question of whether we are ready for and capable of such an about-face. To what extent are we at all able to develop new, basic visions of the totality and to abandon that secret or open materialism that has led to the embarrassing flirtation of Western intelligentsia with the Marxism of which many today no longer wish to hear anything?

[5] R. Guardini, *Die Lebensalter*, 10th ed. (Mainz, 1986), 97. Guardini's entire *oeuvre* is permeated by the confrontation with the idea of progress. The university sermon that he gave in 1956 after the crushing of the Hungarian uprising contains especially penetrating remarks on this subject. I quote only one: "It is false and dangerous to define man as the being that makes progress. No, he is the being that is not protected by any progress, but must always . . . decide anew between good and evil" (in *Wahrheit und Ordnung. Universitätspredigten* 11 [1956], 262).

b. The Forces That Inspired the Revolutionary Change

At this point, we must turn to the practical question of which forces brought about the radical change in the states of Eastern Europe. Here, too, we shall not make political analyses in the narrower sense of the term. After having asked what it was that actually failed and proved to have no future, we now look for what is positive—for the energies that can effect the about-face. Naturally, this cannot be an exhaustive analysis but only a first tentative exploration.

What brought about the revolutionary change? First we must pause in considering the concrete course of the events, so that it becomes meaningful for us to go beyond this. An obvious fact that must be mentioned first as the strongest moving force of the new process is the material failure of the Marxist system in the economic and social realm. In this respect, it has failed in what was most its own—as a theory of economics—and it is no longer to be taken seriously as science today. The intellectual supporters of the system and its functionaries have known this for a long time: faced with the facts, those who embodied the system gradually lost faith in it, so that it had been kept going for a long time, no longer out of conviction, but only through the self-maintenance of power. The lifespan of sheer power, which only clings to itself without being supported by intellectual substance, is necessarily limited. As soon as the "loss of faith" on the part of the powerful coincided with the loss of confidence on the part of those they governed, and with their sheer distress, the brittle structure was bound to begin to shake.

In this context, the power of religion must be mentioned as a second factor. It had been predicted that religion would disappear of its own accord if those societal relationships that had channeled the projection of religion were to change. It had long been admitted that the speed of this process had been overestimated; and then finally more and more the possibility was left open that religion would probably never completely cease to exist altogether. Ultimately, something surprising happened: the question about God arose anew precisely within the intelligentsia of the natural sciences. A science that was becoming aware of its limitations recognized that the real answers lay outside what it in itself could offer. At the same time as the question about God flared up in the midst of the strictest rationality, the thirst for the eternal—which clearly is imprinted in the depths of our soul—made itself heard anew out of the depths of human existence. We know from many testimonies how God became an exciting topic precisely among the young academics who had grown up in a wholly atheistic climate.[6] This did not always

[6] This is attested with special urgency by the writings of T. Goritschewa, cf. esp. *Von Gott zu reden ist gefährlich*, 3d ed.

lead to conversion, to concrete Christian faith. But such questions spontaneously generated, as it were, a new openness to the mysterious message of the icons and the closeness of the divine in the Orthodox liturgy, which is totally consecrated to the *mysterium*. The splendor of religious promises, which had previously paled under the magic of ideological promises, could be felt anew, pointing to other, higher fulfillments of human existence than those that a world deprived of God could offer, such as the substitute solutions of moral libertinism. Religion, which had been seen only a short time before as the embodiment of superstition and oppression, appeared as an agent of freedom; it emerged again as a public force that relativized the dominant power. Religion provided those powers of soul that ultimately became stronger than the external forces.

But we must also think of a third and quite different factor in this process: the influence of the mass media. Here we encounter a strange dichotomy, which we may not omit in the diagnosis of the present hour of history without being guilty of giving an insufficient account of the phenomena. There is no doubt that the mass media have proved to be a

---

(Freiburg, 1984), *Die Kraft der Ohnmächtigen. Weisheit aus dem Leiden* (Wuppertal, 1987). The works of A. Solzhenitsyn, especially *The First Circle* (New York: Harper and Row, 1968), remain important for the path of gradual turning to God.

destabilizing factor with respect to dictatorships. They relativize everything with their skepticism, they show countertypes to everything and thus call everything into question. They present the eye with images of the life one would wish to have and thereby set up a criterion that impels opposition to the existing order. They form the consciousness and the subconscious and urge one to put into practice what has been seen and heard. Thus they have certainly made their contribution to the shaping of a consciousness that was less and less able to accept that the existing order was unchangeable. And they no doubt have their share of merit in what is perhaps the most astonishing and positive aspect of these revolutionary changes: namely, that they took place almost totally without violence. It is indeed true that one must not conceal here the heavy responsibility the mass media (with their banalization of violence, which appears as a quite normal and customary form of human behavior) must assume for the ease with which the threshold to violent action between individuals and groups is crossed over today. But there is another side of their activity, too: whatever happens at one point of the world is seen everywhere, at all places. All the world can see how terrible and cruel the use of military force is against people who demonstrate peacefully, as we saw in China and heard about from Romania. This violence can no longer conceal itself under the mask of action taken to bring about a better society; instead, the brutal face of a bloody dictatorship became visible, chilling the whole world. The world-wide multiplication of images becomes a factor of power in the local event and thereby provides the necessary protection to the defenseless will of those who rise up in protest. These are positive effects of a phenomenon of mass society to which we had not given any thought before. But, without a doubt, another side of this same phenomenon also exists: the power of the images to relativize goes beyond the sphere of dictatorships. They induce a general skepticism. One has the impression that one knows everything and can pass judgment on everything. But this could mean the loss of the ability to perceive the deeper dimensions of existence. We are threatened with a flattening-out of emotions, a grasping for what is external, a claim made on existence that no longer shakes only dictatorships but destabilizes the human soul itself to its very foundations. There is a danger that it may become incapable of the patience that is required to find the truth and incapable of that bond without which the truth does not bestow itself and without which the response of love cannot grow. It is not possible to give a simply negative or a simply positive evaluation of the mass media; precisely in their dichotomy, they are a fateful sign of our times, a sign whose power will develop increasingly in very diverse directions.

2. ANALOGIES AND VARIATIONS
IN THE WESTERN WORLD

Our reflections hitherto have taken their point of departure in the events of Eastern Europe, but we have attempted to reflect at the same time on our own problems too, the problems of the Western world and of its ideologies. In a second section, we must go somewhat more deeply into this aspect of our question, before we can draw conclusions for the direction of faith today.

I should like to address three aspects above all: the crisis of the faith in science, the new question on the spiritual and the ethical, and the new search for religion.

a. The Crisis of the Faith in Science

The resistance of creation to its manipulation by men has become a new factor in the intellectual situation in the last decade. It is impossible to evade the question of the limits of science and of the criteria it must follow. The change in the way in which the case of Galileo is evaluated seems to me characteristic of the change of climate. This event, to which little attention was paid in the seventeenth century, was elevated in the following century to nothing less than the myth of the Enlightenment:

Galileo appears as the victim of the medieval obscurantism in which the Church persists. Good and evil stand in a distinct confrontation: on the one side, we find the Inquisition as the power of superstition, as the opponent of freedom and knowledge; on the other side stand the natural sciences, represented by Galileo, as the power of progress and of the liberation of man from the fetters of ignorance that kept him powerless vis-à-vis nature. The star of the modern period arises over the darkness of the Middle Ages.[7]

Strangely enough, Ernst Bloch with his romantic Marxism was one of the first to oppose this myth openly and to offer a new interpretation of the events. For him, the heliocentric world-system, just like the geocentric system, rests on unprovable presuppositions, including above all the supposition of motionless space, which has since been shattered by the theory of relativity. He states:

> Consequently, since an empty motionless space no longer exists, no movement toward it occurs, but merely a relative movement of bodies toward one another, the determination of which depends on the choice made of the body that is to be taken to be at rest. Thus, if it were not for the fact that the complexity of the calculations involved makes this

[7] Cf. W. Brandmüller, *Galilei und die Kirche oder Das Recht auf Irrtum* (Regensburg, 1982).

appear infeasible, the earth could continue to be taken as stable and the sun as moving.[8]

According to this view, the advantage of the heliocentric system over the geocentric does not consist in a greater degree of objective truth but merely in an easier calculability for us. Up to this point Bloch is doing no more than expressing the insight of the modern natural sciences; but the conclusion he derives from this now is astonishing:

> Since the relativity of the motion is beyond doubt, an older man-centered Christian reference system does not indeed have the right to involve itself in the astronomical calculations and their heliocentric simplification; but it does have its own methodological right to hold fast to the earth as far as the question of the importance of man is concerned and to impart an ordered structure to the world around what happens and has happened on the earth.[9]

The two methodological spheres are clearly distinguished from one another here, and the rights, as well as the limitations, of each are acknowledged. But the summary of the skeptical agnostic philosopher P. Feyerabend sounds much more aggressive when he writes:

[8] E. Bloch, *Das Prinzip Hoffnung* (Frankfurt am Main, 1959), 920; cf. F. Hartl, *Der Begriff des Schöpferischen. Deutungsversuche der Dialektik durch E. Bloch und F. v. Baader* (Frankfurt am Main, 1979), 110.

[9] Bloch, 920f.; Hartl, 111.

The Church at the time of Galileo kept much more closely to reason than did Galileo himself, and she took into consideration the ethical and social consequences of Galileo's teaching too. Her verdict against Galileo was rational and just, and the revision of this verdict can be justified only on grounds of what is politically opportune. [10]

C. F. von Weizsäcker (to take one example) goes even one step farther in considering the practical effects when he sees a "perfectly straight path" leading from Galileo to the atomic bomb. To my surprise, when I was interviewed recently about the case of Galileo, I was not asked (for instance) why the Church had presumed to hinder the knowledge of the natural sciences but, quite to the contrary, why the Church had not taken up a clearer position against the disasters that were bound to result when Galileo opened Pandora's box. It would be foolish to construct an impulsive apologetic on the basis of such views; faith does not grow out of resentment and skepticism with respect to rationality, but only out of a fundamental affirmation and a spacious reasonableness; we shall come back to this point. I mention all this only as a symptomatic case that permits us to see how deep the self-doubt of the modern age, of science and of technology goes today.

[10] P. Feyerabend, *Wider den Methodenzwang* (Frankfurt am Main, 1976, 1983), 206.

b. The Search for the Spiritual and the Ethical

Let us now turn to a second area, that of the new search for an ethos and for "spirituality". Just as it is not possible to give an exclusively positive or exclusively negative evaluation of the doubts regarding science and the modern age that are spreading today, so it is not possible to portray the new openness to the spiritual dimension of the world and of human existence as a uniform phenomenon. Naturally, there is an unequivocally positive course of events today: if the moral was relegated entirely to the subjective realm at the height of the modern age, and technological progress was seen in itself as an unquestionable value, today the question about the ethical as the criterion of our activity has emerged anew in the same circles. To see ethical criteria as a boundary limiting what we research and what we do is no longer condemned a priori as obscurantism, since first the atomic bomb and then the life-destroying forms produced by technology have permitted the obverse side of progress to be perceived in practice. The effect of such a fundamental insight still continues for the most part, of course, to be limited in the practical sphere, as we see in the controversy about genetic manipulation and the procreation of man *in vitro*. The willingness to use human life—the life of persons, even if these are unborn—for the "higher ends" of research or for other goals considered to be good continues undiminished. The use of man as a thing, and playing with the divine mystery of his being, still goes on as before. But there is opposition, even—and precisely—within the ranks of the natural sciences.[11]

c. New Religiosity

Finally, the rediscovery of the religious dimension, too, is many-sided. Just as there is a decisive new turning to the ethical problem and a rejection of the self-satisfaction of positivism precisely among the outstanding minds of the modern natural sciences, so there is an awakening of young people today, who are asking passionately about God, ready to let their life be determined totally and fundamentally by him. There is a greater generosity on the part of young people, who are not satisfied with vague feelings and half-hearted decisions but who seek unconditional obedience to the truth. Besides this, however, there is a widespread, rather vague tendency that one could call a yearning for spirituality and for religious

[11] For a noteworthy new starting point, cf. C. Labrusse-Riou, "L'Homme à vif: biotechnologie et droits de l'homme", in *Esprit*, 156 (Nov. 1989), 60–70. On this, cf. the urgent voice of H. Jonas, "Technik, Ethik und Biogenetische Kunst", in *Internat. kath. Zeitschrift* 13 (1984), 501–17. Cf. also R. Löw (ed.), *Bioethik* (Cologne, 1990).

experience. It would be wrong to dismiss this, but it would also be inappropriate to see in it the beginning of a new turning to the Christian faith. For this yearning often arises from a disappointment at the shortcomings of the technological world; it contains nostalgic elements and above all a deep skepticism with regard to man's vocation to truth. Truth seems to be discredited in history by the intolerance of those who fancied themselves in secure possession of it. Besides this, the experience of the limitations of science and the weakness of ideologies provokes skepticism rather than encourages the search for truth. Thus truth tends to be replaced by "values" about which one can seek at least a partial agreement. But such a selection remains questionable if the criterion of truth is inaccessible. But above all, religion, if it is born of skepticism and disappointment at the boundaries of knowledge, necessarily becomes the domain of the irrational. It remains in the sphere of the nonbinding and easily turns into a narcotic. New mythologies are formed, as we see with particular clarity in the many-faceted phenomenon that is offered up for sale under the collective name "New Age". The parallels to the gnosis of the ancient world are striking: in both, abstruse themes of mythology are linked to the ambitious claim to possess the key of knowledge and to have found an all-embracing interpretation of reality, in which the mysteries of the universe are uncovered and knowledge becomes redemption.[12] The living God sinks down into the spiritual depths of existence in which man bathes and ultimately is dissolved in order to become one with the All out of which he has come. Karl Barth's observation that religion can become a kind of self-satisfying process that does not lead to God, but rather confirms man in himself and closes him against God, takes on a new contemporary relevance.

3. Paths of Faith Today

At the conclusion, we now ask explicitly the question that has silently accompanied all our reflections up to this point: What ought we to do? What can provide a human future that is worth living? When we review the forces we have discussed hitherto, we can reduce them to two fundamental orientations: relativism and faith. Relativism unites easily with positivism; it is indeed positivism's own philosophical basis. We do not wish to dispute the fact that in many situations a dash of relativism, a bit of skepticism, can be useful; but it certainly does not suffice as a common ground on which we can live. For where

[12] For material on this complex of questions, cf. P. Beyerhaus and L. E. von Padberg (eds.), *Eine Welt—Eine Religion? Die synkretistische Bedrohung unseres Glaubens im Zeichen von New Age* (Asslar, 1988).

PATHS OF FAITH IN REVOLUTIONARY CHANGE 103

relativism is consistently thought through and lived
(without clinging secretly to an ultimate trust that
comes from faith), either it becomes nihilism or else
it expands positivism into the power that dominates
everything, thus ending once again in totalitarian
conditions. But what is left, if skepticism and relativism—despite all their partial usefulness—are not, on
the whole, a path? Are we not directed anew to man's
self-transcendence, to the path of faith in the living
God?

A thousand objections are raised today to such an
answer; all the pitiful forms of faith that have been
produced in the past and in the present seem to justify these objections. The courage to believe cannot
be communicated today, as formerly, in a purely intellectual manner. It requires first and foremost witnesses who verify faith as the correct path through
their living and their suffering. The fact that faith
became the force in Eastern Europe that proved to be
stronger than "scientific socialism" is due in fact primarily to the humility and the patience of those who
suffered, in whom the witness to a greater promise
became visible. In this respect, our question goes far
beyond a merely intellectual debate. But it is indis-
pensable and has its own irreplaceable function.

This is why we must now go on to ask, vis-à-vis
the caricatures and perversions of faith: What is the
essential inner form of faith? Or, in other words:
What must constitute a faith that responds to the

signs of the times and thus shows man the path to
redemption in this hour? I should like to propose
three trains of thought.

a. Faith Is Reasonable

Faith is not the resignation of reason in view of the
limits of our knowledge; it is not a retreat into the
irrational in view of the dangers of a merely instru-
mental reason. Faith is not the expression of weari-
ness and flight but is courage to exist and an
awakening to the greatness and breadth of what is
real. Faith is an act of affirmation; it is based on the
power of a new Yes, which becomes possible for man
when he is touched by God. It seems to me important, precisely amid the rising resentment against
technical rationality, to emphasize clearly the essential
reasonableness of faith. In a criticism of the modern
period, which has long been going on, one must not
reproach its confidence in reason as such but only the
narrowing of the concept of reason, which has
opened the door to irrational ideologies. But the *mysterium*, as faith sees it, is not the irrational but rather
the uttermost depths of the divine reason, which our
weak eyes are no longer able to penetrate. It is and
remains a fundamental word of faith when John—
taking up and deepening the creation narrative of the
Old Testament—begins his Gospel with the words:
"In the beginning was the Logos", the creative rea-

son, the power of the divine knowledge that imparts meaning. It is only from this beginning that one can correctly understand the mystery of Christ, in which reason can then be seen to be the same as love. The first word of faith, therefore, tells us: everything that exists is thought that has poured forth. The Creator Spirit is the origin and the supporting foundation of all things. Everything that is, is reasonable in terms of its origin, for it comes from creative reason.

Here, once again, we are confronted with the fundamental antithesis between materialism and faith. The creed of materialism is that the irrational stands at the beginning and that only the laws of chance have constructed the rational out of the irrational. Thus, reason is a by-product of the irrational; it is a mere assemblage in its laws, without any ethical or aesthetic content. This makes man in turn the assembler of the world, which he designs according to the criteria of his goals. But the real primal force always remains the irrational. For faith, it is exactly the opposite: the Spirit is the creative origin of all things, and therefore they all bear reason in themselves; this reason does not come from them but infinitely transcends them, yet it forms the law of their being. The creative reason that creates the objective reasonableness of things, their hidden mathematics and their inner order, is at the same time moral reason, and it is love. Man exists in order to recognize the traces of this reason and so to develop things in keeping with their essence. His rule is a service, and his freedom is a bond, namely, to the inner truth of things, and thus openness for the love that makes him like God.

The modern period is marked by a strange oscillation between rationalism and irrationality. Considering this dichotomy, it seems important to me to characterize the alternatives correctly. The fundamental alternative before which the course of the modern period sets us consists in the question: Does the irrational stand at the beginning of all things, is the irrational the real origin of the world, or does it come from creative reason? To believe means to take the second alternative, and only this is "reasonable", in the deepest sense of the word, and worthy of man. In the crisis of reason that confronts us today, this real essence of faith must once again become visible, this essence that saves reason, precisely because it grasps reason in its whole breadth and depth and protects it from the restrictions of a merely experiential verification. The *mysterium* is not opposed to reason but saves and defends the reasonableness of existence and of man.

b. The Cooperation of Thinking, Willing and Feeling in Faith

Let us now turn from the realm of knowledge to that of willing and feeling. A fundamental preliminary decision has already been made here through our previous reflections. Schleiermacher attempted to save religion, in the fundamental danger to which the Enlightenment exposed it, by defining religion as feeling: "Its essence is neither thinking nor acting but intuition and feeling." [13] "Praxis is art, speculation is science, religion is sensitivity and taste for the infinite." [14] The nineteenth century largely followed him in this and found in this way its own kind of reconciliation between religion and science: reason could do as it liked; religion, which was wholly feeling, did not stand in its way and was for its own part free to express itself in the realm of feeling and to make its own position secure. The danger of such an intellectual truce still exists today; but this is not a peace but rather a division of man in which reason and feeling suffer equal damage.

It is in fact a resignation on the part of reason when it considers itself capable only of what is functional, no longer knows itself to be competent to recognize the truth of existence, the truth about us, about creation and about God. But this skepticism holds the field today to a large extent. We no longer dare for the most part to presume that we could recognize truth in the essence of our questioning. This false humility abases man, making our action blind

[13] F. Schleiermacher, *Über die Religion. Reden an die Gebildeten unter ihren Verächtern* (Berlin, 1799; quoted from the edition by H.-J. Tothert published by F. Meiner, Hamburg, 1958), 29.
[14] Ibid., 30.

and our feeling empty. Even in the Catholic Church, one rarely hears the claim any more that the truth about God becomes visible to us in faith. The impression is spreading that all religions grope in darkness and that all their statements are symbols of what is utterly unknowable. Thus religion is becoming once again a sphere of higher feelings. The religions, which have become interchangeable, are to serve the noblest goals of mankind with the thrust of the best feelings and to be instruments for the construction of a society of universal peace.

It is of course true that we all wish for universal peace. It is a justified imperative that to look toward God allows us to recognize men as our brothers and sisters and thus serves peace. But a religion that is nothing more than a means to attain particular goals is debased just as much as a religion that is allowed to govern only as feeling.[15] All errors contain truths. It is true that religion summons to peace; it is true that feeling, too, belongs to religion and that reforms that remove the humus of feelings will not succeed. But these truths retain their power only when they do not lose their own inherent interconnection. This interconnection consists in the fact that faith takes up feeling and redeems it from its indeterminacy by giving it its true ground: the feeling for the infinite is

[15] On these tendencies, cf. the clear-sighted presentation by R. Slenczka, "Das Forum 'Gerechtigkeit, Frieden und Bewahrung der Schöpfung'", in *Kerygma und Dogma* 35 (1989), 316–35.

based on the truth that there exists an infinite God and that he addresses us, the finite ones. One will not restore power to faith today by reducing it as much as possible to the indeterminate but only by seeing it in its entire magnitude. Reduction does not save faith; it cheapens it. It becomes meaningful only when one leaves it its entire power. Then it is no longer we who save faith but faith that saves us.

c. The Personal and Social Character of Faith

The integration of knowledge, will and feeling takes place in the person. Christian faith has essentially a personal structure. It is the answer of a person to a personal call. It is the encounter of two freedoms. We have already said that Christian faith, on the basis of its essence as described in the Bible, is not irrationalism but is the most decisive declaration that reason is the ground and goal of all things; we can now add that Christian faith in its essence includes a comprehensive philosophy of freedom. All we need do here, really, is repeat from another aspect what we have said above about the fundamental alternatives of thought. We noted that modern rationalism, on the basis of its methodological self-limitation, declares the irrational to be the origin of the rational. This means that it must declare the basis of freedom to be that which is not free, that is, that freedom, like reason, is a by-product of the self-construction of the world. Against this, faith, which knows the Logos as the beginning, has the primacy of freedom as its starting point. Only the link to the Logos guarantees freedom as the structural principle of what really exists.

This has disadvantages, in terms of the theory of systems: philosophies of what is necessary assert that they can explain everything. They offer user's instructions on how to bring about the better world by necessity. The philosophy of freedom that comes from faith cannot do this. It has no simple formula for the world. Or, to put it more exactly, its formula for the world is the freedom of God's love, which calls us in Jesus Christ and ever anew shows the path for man's freedom.

The effects of this reach into practical forms of piety. An apersonal piety corresponds to an apersonal philosophy. It cannot be denied that tendencies of this kind exist among Christians: there is a disintegration of the courage to believe in the personal God who hears us. Thus piety becomes a process of letting oneself sink down into the stream of being, redemption from the burden of freedom, from the burden of being a person, a return into the abyss of nothingness. Christian praying, however, is the response one freedom makes to another freedom, an encounter of love. Once again, the tendency to apersonal piety bears a portion of truth in itself: it seeks to overcome the difference that separates us from the Other and from others. But the withdrawal of existence, the resignation that this contains, does not save. The difference is overcome precisely when the encounter of two freedoms becomes love. It is not the denial of the person but rather the person's highest act, namely, love, that creates that unity for which we yearn from the depths of our existence, as creatures of the triune God.[16]

Thus we can say in closing: faith is no comfortable path. Anyone who offers faith as a comfortable path will not succeed. It makes the highest demands of man, because it thinks highly of him. But precisely because it does this, it is beautiful and in keeping with our own being. If we see it in its whole magnitude and breadth, then it bears in itself the answers for which our hour of history is calling.

[16] On this, cf. Congregation for the Doctrine of the Faith, "Letter to the Bishops of the Catholic Church on Certain Aspects of Christian Meditation" (Vatican City, 1989; English edition: San Francisco: Ignatius Press, 1990). Still worth reading, on this question, is J. A. Cuttat, *Asiatische Gottheit—Christlicher Gott. Die Spiritualität der beiden Hemisphären* (Einsiedeln, 1971; French original, 1965).

II

EUROPE—HOPES AND DANGERS*

PRELIMINARY REFLECTIONS:
PHENOMENOLOGY OF TODAY'S EUROPE

The idea of Europe has fallen into a strange twilight today. It had its great hour in the moment of distress, when the nationalism that had been intensified to the point of ideological madness had laid waste the countries of the old continent. Then people began to reflect again on the common roots, on the common culture that had grown in a process of mutual exchanges, on the ethical and religious patrimony, on the rationality of this culture and on its power to create unity. In that situation, Europe became the expression of the common, unifying element that existed prior to the divisions and that these divisions had never been able to extinguish completely. Thus

* A lecture given as part of the celebrations of the two-thousandth anniversary of the city of Speyer. I have deliberately wished to let the conclusion, with its reference to this specific context, stand as it is here, as a concrete exemplification of the idea of Europe.

the idea of Europe proved its worth as a positive moral power in the period after the War. It became the seal of reconciliation after the madness of destruction: it made possible an ordered peace between those who had once been enemies, it allowed the world to become more open and larger for the individual, and at the same time it gave economic well-being, indeed, power. Europe—a word for peace and reconciliation: this is the great and positive element in our epoch's experience of Europe. This aspect of Europe is making itself heard anew today, now that the doors between East and West have opened. Their reconciliation had never been totally blocked by the Iron Curtain after the War but had had to stop at the half-way point. The search for the complete realization of this reconciliation in a viable political and economic form is taking ·place today once again under the sign of the common membership in Europe. The countries of the West, which have drawn close together, are confronted with the challenge of finding new forms of unity in multiplicity and of conceiving a new order for peace over a huge area. The old anxieties of the nationalistic epoch make themselves heard anew in the debate about the reunification of Germany. Boundaries appear once again in their immovable significance; the antithetical character of nationalism could become stronger than the European fellowship that has scarcely begun to grow. It must be demonstrated

anew whether Europe is only an idea or a real power
for reconciliation. It must be demonstrated anew
whether the inner unity of history and culture, of
task and responsibility, is strong enough to give
boundaries a better meaning than that of separation.
It becomes easier to respect boundaries, the more
they are at the same time open paths; the more
minorities on each side can live their own lives as a
totality; the more a living exchange, a recognized
plurality and common fellowship in this plurality
dominate everywhere, so that exclusiveness is not
found anywhere. No sane person today can want
new expulsions to take place in Europe, with new
boundary shifts. But ethical and political common
sense demands just as much that boundaries become
points of exchange and that they no longer be permitted to be armed symbols of the absolutization of a
national principle.

Thus, the turning point of 1989 has given a new
impetus to the idea of Europe too. It seemed from
the 1970s onward that the great program of reconciliation and of a new ethical beginning summarized in
the word "Europe" would be slowly but surely
smothered in the thickets of the economic bureau-
cracy, but the tearing down of the Iron Curtain has
renewed in one stroke the original challenge: our
common location in the ethical entity that is Europe
must lead to a new order for peace, to an exchange
of the gifts of the spirit and of the earth. Europe, as a

political idea, must finally replace the model of the
nation state with a generous concept of cultural fellowship, with a solidarity that embraces all of mankind taking the place of errors committed along the
path of nationalism. For it is not mutual opposition
but rather coexistence that builds up the individual
nations too.

In this reflection we have already heard the two
themes that have for some time raised doubts about
the validity of the idea of Europe. The first was the
increasing decline of the European idea into a merely
economic arithmetic that did indeed continually increase Europe's economic power in the world but
reduced the great ethical goals more and more to an
increase of possessions and lowered them to the level
of the mere logic of the market. The consequence of
this within Europe itself had already been a kind of
cultural revolution: a standardization not only of
merchandise but also of intellectual expression,
which threatens to lead to a flattening of souls and a
uniformity in thinking to an extent hitherto unknown. Established cultural forms collapse; the over-
powering maelstrom of big anonymous structures
leads in agriculture, in trade and in small businesses to
a loss of personal freedom of organization for which
is substituted the fake glitter of a world in which
freedom knows no ethical restrictions.

What happened inside Europe itself displayed its
truly tragic countenance all the more clearly in the

non-European world, in the southern half of the globe. The change in the ethical evaluation of the new Europe after the War became obvious as soon as the increasing possession of power replaced the previous efforts toward reconciliation. Initially, development aid could count as a moral justification of one's own wealth; it seemed to be only a question of time before the "miracle" of Europe would spread in this way to the rest of the world, to unite North and South in the same system of well-being. The fact that both East and West at this same time wanted to export (each in its own way) their "happiness" to the rest of the world, thereby also transporting their antagonism there, was only *one* reason for the failure of this undertaking. The causes of this failure lay also in the purely mechanical concept of the increase of prosperity, and therefore in the way in which they interpreted "happiness" for others and consequently practiced development aid. The fact is that economic aid, in the forms given, did not produce a gradual advancement of wholly different living conditions but instead brought about real distress. The export of what was European and American did indeed profit the countries that gave, but it impoverished the countries that received. Instead of unity, it created anger and misery. Thus self-doubt increased within Europe. Europe's own wealth led to feelings of guilt. Eurocentrism became a term of reproach, and the history of Europe's triumphs became now a history of its falls. Even as late as the preceding generation, Paul Claudel could write his *Christopher Columbus* as the drama of the liberation of South America from its bloody gods, as the path to the unity of mankind in the humaneness of the Christian faith, which overcomes the particularism and the inhumanity of superstitious cults. Who would dare today to portray the entry of the Europeans into the South American hemisphere in such a way? There are many who think that the opposite should have happened: Europe should have been freed from Christianity and from the claim to superiority that it deduces from its certainty of possessing the truth. But even those who do not go as far as that are unable to see in the Spanish conquest much of anything more than yet another history of violent oppression, a history full of greed and cruelty for which even the humble service of so many great missionaries cannot compensate. The celebration of the five-hundredth anniversary of the first encounter between Europe and America, which is now being prepared in Latin America, is marked by such questions. After the fateful voyage of Columbus, Europe has stretched out to America and has (so to speak) presented itself there once again. Was this a blessing or a curse for America, and for Europe itself? It will be a difficult task to draw up the accounts of one or the other and to balance them against each other. In any case, Europe must take to its very soul the warning not to repeat a Eurocentrism that has crushed and destroyed so much in Africa and in Asia too, with its foolish self-certainty.

This broad outline of the fate and effects of the idea of Europe in the second half of our century allows us to see two antithetical aspects of the phenomenon of Europe. On the one hand, we have Europe as idea and as power for reconciliation, leading out of the nationalistic epoch and opening up a new model of fellowship between peoples; on the other hand, Europe appears as a claim to sovereignty and as an economic power that collects other things and other people—that is, reduces or even destroys other people's personal rights and their own way of life. Europe moves between these two poles. It must learn to distinguish between its danger and its true greatness: the question of whether Europe's name becomes a blessing or a curse depends on this.

Hence, our question is: What must Europe do to fulfill its positive mission? What must it stop, so as not to fall from its true being [*Wesen*] into its ever-possible evil ways [*Unwesen*]? I should like to approach the answer in two steps. Up to now we have contented ourselves with a kind of phenomenology of what is European, that is, with a look at how the idea of Europe works today and how it is seen by others. Now we must go somewhat more deeply and come to an examination of conscience; we must ask: What are the essential mistakes of Europe that have brought it to the prisoner's dock today? How can one recognize these mistakes, and how can one distinguish them from Europe's greatness, its valid contribution to the history of mankind? The second step consists in the transition from the examination of conscience to the search for the path, that is, to the question of what Europe ought to be and to do.

1. Europe's Two Falls from Grace in the Modern Period

a. Nationalism

Let us therefore begin with the first question: What are the sins of Europe and of Europeans that must at all costs not be repeated or allowed to continue? It would certainly not be difficult to draw up a long catalogue of errors. I should like to summarize what is negative in two great keywords, which, moreover, concentrate on what is presently at work or threatening, and thus refer in a narrower sense to the Europe of the modern period, which arose after the French Revolution. I should like to summarize the first complex of errors under the keyword "nationalism", which has already been mentioned frequently. This is not a wholly new sin; it is merely the modern radicalization of tribalism, one of mankind's primal vices. Tribalism stands as a disaster in archaic history, and its bloody trail crosses the centuries. But this ancient vice takes on a new dimension in the European nationalism of the nineteenth and twentieth centuries, in a twofold manner. The structure of the nation grew in the course of the Middle Ages and the early modern period in a complicated process of cultural and political assimilation within areas ethnically related to one another. It presents itself clearly for the first time in the French Revolution, in which monarchic unity is replaced by national unity. In the course of the nineteenth century, Germany and Italy constituted themselves as nations, while in Spain and Great Britain the long history of a world-wide colonial expansion had allowed a corresponding awareness of distinctness and of mission to come to maturity. Poland, too, became aware of itself as a nation in the uprisings of the nineteenth century; in Russia, it was not least the Slavophile theology that had formed the idea of a theophoric people and thereby a Russian national consciousness with a religious stamp. In Central Europe, after a German national state had taken shape under the propulsion of Prussia, Austro-Hungary had received a final configuration that was not based on the national principle. The chief political result of the First World War was the liquidation of this final remnant of an earlier polity and the attempt finally to restructure Europe strictly in terms of the national idea—a process full of inherent contradictions, which then found its dreadful finale in the paroxysm of the national socialistic madness.

But what was new in this principle of construction? First of all, a mythical exaltation of one's own nation took place to a greater or lesser extent among the European peoples. Each of them now considered itself to be the criterion for the realization of what was genuinely humane and therefore claimed the right to bring to bear its own way of life, and thus its power, in the rest of the world. One could speak of a strange union between nationalism and universalism: the unity of the world was to be born under the sign of one's own nation; it was to be based on the priority of what was one's own, not on the balance of the whole. The phrase "God with us" expressed an appropriation of what was holy, attempting to mobilize the forces of Christianity for the national interest. One's own Christianity was seen as purer; Harnack had given the classic presentation of this in his comparison of the three fundamental forms of Christianity—the Roman, the Germanic and the Byzantine-Slavic.[1] (Let us only add parenthetically that the pride of Germanic Christianity vis-à-vis Roman and Slavic Christianity remains unbroken even today and continues to have its effect as myth even when the religious substance has been lost, favoring emotions that block the path to unity.) This

[1] A. von Harnack, *Das Wesen des Christentums* (1900), jubilee ed. (Stuttgart, 1950), 113–17.

mythologizing of the national had attained its own explosive force by uniting itself with belief in progress and with the myth of the technical world. According to this, the form of life of one's own nation showed the path indicated by progress; all the others appeared to have made less progress and therefore had to follow on the same path. The power of the economic-technical civilization gave the conflicts that were thus programmed their world-wide destructive violence; it allowed the archaic tribalistic impulse, with its pseudorationality, to become a threat to mankind. In this context, one would have to speak of colonialism and of its export of European wars into the far parts of the earth; one would also have to take into consideration the new dimension of slavery, which was developed in the context of the great discoveries of the early modern period and now rests as a burden of guilt on European and American history.

b. The Exclusiveness of Technical Reason and the Destruction of the Ethos

The idea of Europe was formulated after the Second World War in order to banish the nationalistic heresy once and for all and to attain a new political principle aimed, not at mutual exclusion, but at complementarity and cooperation. Although nationalism was born in Europe and in this sense is a European heresy, we may nevertheless look on the renewed idea of Europe as a powerful antidote to this false path of our history and decisively oppose all attempts at regression. Although the danger of nationalism has not been overcome easily, it is not—we hope—the real temptation of our period. This temptation has its basis in a second fall from grace, which we must now attempt to investigate thoroughly: we mean the union—already heard in the extreme forms of nationalism—between belief in progress, the absolutization of the scientific-technical civilization and the promise of the new humanity, of the messianic kingdom. There is no doubt that it was in Marxism that this threefold association was most consistently developed into a political myth of almost irresistible power. This is why not a few European intellectuals are at a loss, since they must now attempt to get along without it, especially since their own consciousness of innocence and the clarity of the assignment of guilt were closely bound to this mythological synthesis. It is not possible at present to foresee to what extent there will be restorations of Marxism in this intellectual climate; a need for such restorations might arise because of the fact that Marxism appeared to replace the lost Christian faith with a dynamic of hope that had already set itself up as a kind of post-Christian religion. For the time being, we can but hope that the pain of those who have been set free, everything that they have suffered and gone through, may speak to the world with sufficient urgency to prevent any farther-reaching forms of restoration.

If, however, we are to benefit from what has happened, we must of course be aware that Marxism was only the radical execution of an ideological concept that even without Marxism largely determines the signature of our century. We have earlier attempted to grasp its political and historical essence by portraying it as the connection of belief in progress with absolutized scientific-technical civilization and political messianism. The remarkable thing about this strange trinity is, however, that this structure now replaces the concept of God and necessarily excludes it, since it takes its place. This systematic exclusion of the divine from the shaping of history and human life, referring to the definitiveness of scientific insight, is perhaps the genuinely new, and at the same time the truly threatening, element in that strange product of Europe that we call Marxism. I now assert that this same combination, in weaker forms, is active in the life of the Western world even outside Marxist thinking. If it were to succeed in establishing itself definitively, this would, on the one hand, be Eurocentrism in the bad sense of the word, but, on the other hand, simultaneously, it would also be the end of what could make Europe a positive force in the world.

It will immediately be objected that the resentment against technology and science is spreading more and more today and that belief in progress has long since given way to a resigned skepticism. But resentment and skepticism are not foundations on which to build; they are no good at overcoming ideas. One can move beyond ideas only through a larger and better affirmation, not through negations and halfheartedness. Actually, technology and science will continue to develop with an immanent necessity in the future, too, and their transmission is likewise the logical consequence of their universality. This cannot be limited by the romantic dream of abiding pretechnological paradises, dreams that are employed to forbid others to have something we ourselves would not care to do without. Better means must be found to limit the damage they cause. But the continued course of technological development will ensure that the belief in progress does not die out and thereby that political messianism, too, remains alive in changing forms: for surely it must be possible at some time, in some way, to create at last the better world and the new man—who dares to revoke this dream, which has in the meantime become the true hope and consolation of mankind? One who does this would look today somewhat as the atheist did in earlier times: one who denies what actually keeps the world running. But both of these, technological progress and the belief that the new world can be constructed on its basis, quite logically involve the view that one must leave God out of

what happens in history and assign the question of
his existence and of who he is entirely to the realm
of the private (and thus the arbitrary). In this sense,
the realm of religion becomes the genuine place
where tolerance reigns: religion's sacred principle
must above all be that it does not step out of this tol-
erated area of what is merely private and does not lay
claim to any rights in public life. But all this means
that Europe will export technical skills without
ethos, and ultimately against ethos; that the superior
force of the ideology of technological progress will
destroy those great ethical traditions on which the
old societies were based, while the dark practices of
sorcery and magic continue to exist or even gain
stronger influence. It also means that the spirit of
having and making things, along with the escape into
the empty promise of a "tomorrow", will fill the
whole world. It means a unity of mankind that
extinguishes at the same time the forces that truly
unite it and the great fundamental ethical convictions
that mankind has in common. Robert Spaemann has
given a precise formulation to the question at issue
here:

> Can Europe . . . accept the responsibility for the
> destruction of all traditional cultures through the
> universalization of the scientific objectification of
> the world and the goal-oriented rational organiza-
> tion of life, while retaining for itself the only thing
> that can . . . compensate for this destruction: the

idea of the unconditional? This idea, in its essence
and origin, is the idea of God.[2]

The consequences of the destruction of ethical
foundations are in fact becoming dramatically visible
today in the epidemic spread of a civilization of
death. Narcotics are the attempt to anticipate already
today a world that can be built only in the future.
This is perfectly logical, since none of the builders
will experience this world himself. So he must open
up this world for himself in advance, by other means.
The countries that live off the production of drugs
are linked to those who consume them by a highway
of death that becomes wider and wider and needs less
and less to conceal itself. Terrorism needs no ideological excuse today; it reveals itself nakedly as the
self-evident fact of violence that justifies itself
through its successes. Robber bands challenge the
state and can establish themselves as a kind of coun-
terstate. Besides this, we have already experienced
the next step in our century: namely, states that have
fallen into the hands of robber bands. This was especially obvious in Hitler's *Reich* but incontestably also
where a gulag archipelago became the expression of
the state's oppressive power.

[2] R. Spaemann, "Universalismus oder Eurozentrismus?", in
K. Michalski (ed.), *Europa und die Folgen* (Stuttgart, 1988), 313–
22, particularly 320f.

2. Diagnosis on the Basis of Historical Roots

a. What Distinguishes the State from the Well-Led Robber Band?

This makes it clear what a false Eurocentrism is. But how can this be overcome? And what can and ought Europe truly to be and to give? The approach to this reflection opens up when we examine somewhat more closely the keyword "state as robber band" and endeavor to grasp the precise distinction between a well-organized society of robbers and a true state. It was Seneca—Nero's tutor, who later became the martyr of his tyranny—who first said that states without justice are nothing but vast, overgrown bands of robbers.[3] We find this again in Tacitus, and again on the lips of the Stoic martyr who replied, when the Emperor Commodus asked him why he denied him the acknowledgment of his divinity as emperor that he had granted to Commodus' father, Marcus Aurelius: "That was appropriate in the case of . . . your father, who was a wise and perfect man, but not in your case, since you are a tyrant and chief of a robber band." [4]

This expression has thus acquired its concrete meaning through the practical experience of rulers

[3] E. von Ivánka, *Rhomäerreich und Gottesvolk* (Freiburg, 1968), 17.

[4] Ibid., 17f.

who were in reality robbers. But its philosophical presuppositions lie deeper. The consideration of these leads us to the heart of the Greek and Roman philosophy of the state, in which Europe's intellectual roots lie: the criteria of what is good and the threat of its corruption. The oldest root that can be discerned is a pre-Socratic doctrine of three realms, where the peoples are classified according to their characters and their geographical zones. The peoples in the North are characterized by warlike wildness, but also by an individualistic unruliness, so that an ordered social life and the construction of genuine states are not found there. In the peoples of the East and the South reign dissipation, servility and political indolence, so that they easily let themselves be subjugated by despots, in spite of their science, their artistic skill, their business zeal and their ability in trade. Finally, in the temperate zone—in Hellas—we find the right balance between militant courage and peaceful talents, so that the true *polis* is realized here "where the order of the state does not suffocate the freedom of the individual, nor unchecked independence shatter the structure of the state".[5]

Plato's great achievement was to remove this scheme of three states from the geographical division and to link it instead with the three fundamental modes of human existence, thus uniting politics to anthropology. He speaks of three parts of the soul in

[5] Ibid., 35–42, particularly 37.

man, but we can instead speak simply of three fundamental modes of man's integration or disintegration.
The form of the state will depend on which of these
three fundamental anthropological forms wins the
upper hand. We have the reign of that which is low-
est in man—the reign of lust, the lust for possessions,
for power, for pleasure. Reason and heart become
instruments to serve what is lower; man sees in
another only a rival or an instrument for the exten-
sion of his own ego. Market forces and public opinion dominate man and become the caricature of
freedom. All that stands above lust in Plato's anthropological formula is the naked will, the audacity of
daring and of undertaking; but this remains blind. For
Plato, the true location of man's integration is the
nous, a word that we translate very inadequately as
reason or understanding. What is meant is the ability
to perceive the true criteria of Being itself, the organ
that perceives the divine.[6] It is only through this act,
whereby man reaches out beyond himself, that the
integration of the individual in himself and with himself, as well as the integration of society, takes place.
Men cannot really be united by a common interest
but only by the truth; in this way, freedom and justice
are brought to realization in their inherent unity.[7]

[6] Ibid., 38.

[7] In this context, I should like to draw attention to the
significant work by the Czech philosopher J. Patocka, *Platon et
l'Europe* (Paris, 1983), written in the midst of oppression by the

Here we can state with a fair amount of precision what the distinction is between a large group of robbers and a genuine state: merely pragmatic criteria, which are thereby necessarily the criteria of a party, determined by the group, are essentially the constitutive factor of structured robber societies. Something other than these—that is, something other than a large group that regulates itself only in accordance with its goals—exists only when a righteousness comes into play that is measured, not by the interest of the group, but by a universal criterion. Only this do we call the "justice" that constitutes the state. It includes the Creator and creation as its points of orientation. This means that a state that is in principle agnostic vis-à-vis God and constructs justice only on the basis of majority opinions inherently sinks down to the level of the robber band. In this, one must simply accept as correct Augustine's definitive interpretation of the Platonic tradition: where God is

communist dictatorship, which refers back very deliberately to Plato and interprets him as the father of Europe—of what Europe should be—because of his fundamental preoccupation with the "care for the soul". Patocka finds in Plato three levels on which the "care for the soul" is exercised: first the emergence from the intimacy and the withdrawnness of the consciousness to take one's place in reality, as this is carried out by Platonic metaphysics; then the ethical-political level, and, as third level, finally, the ethical-religious. Cf. also A. Rigobello, "Platone 'padre' dell' idea d'Europa", *Osservatore Romano*, April 27, 1990, 3.

excluded, the principle of the robber band exists, in variously harsher or milder forms. This begins to become visible where the organized killing of innocent human beings—unborn human beings—is clothed with the appearance of right, because it is protected by the interest of a majority.[8]

b. Progress and Regress

We must return again briefly to Plato and to the classical philosophy of the state. As we have seen, Plato transformed the scheme of three kingdoms into an anthropological scheme, but he conceived of this at the same time as a cyclical historical scheme: for him, this is the formula of historical decadence. In keeping with an inherent law of life, states descend from the first stage to the second, and so to the third. Despite this, Plato is no pessimist: for him, this is not a linear historical course but a process that repeats itself ever anew. After each fall, history begins again at the beginning with different subjects. It has no definitive direction; it is a cycle of repetitions. Each ascent is followed by a descent, and vice versa; no political structure will last forever, and none is the final stage of history. Originally, the Romans also held this view; in the republican period, they did not in the least expect Rome to last forever. Sallust says expli-

[8] Augustine, *City of God* IV, 4 (C. Chr. XLVII, 101); on this, J. Ratzinger, *Die Einheit der Nationen* (Salzburg, 1971), 71–103.

citly that everything that has come into being also perishes.[9]

The philosophy of the imperial period in Rome sees this differently: it takes up biblical ideas and expands the scheme of the three kingdoms to the idea of four kingdoms, the last of which—Rome—is immortal and the true fulfillment of man's communal development. The cyclical scheme is replaced by the linear, which no longer contains any decline: it constructs history as progress that has attained its goal in Rome. The belief in progress had been acquired, which, naturally, met with opposition from those who had to suffer under Roman dominion and who therefore were unable to recognize it as the goal of history.[10]

It would be fascinating to examine the synthesis in which Augustine, after the sack of Rome by the West Goths in the year 410, when all the signs threatened a coming destruction, blended the Platonic and Roman tradition on the basis of the new elements of the Christian faith. By uniting cyclical and linear, ascending and descending considerations of history, he corrected their one-sidednesses and thus created the intellectual foundations on which Europe could

[9] Ivánka, 40ff.; on Sallust, 45, n. 84.

[10] Ibid., 39f.; cf., on the whole issue, also A. A. I. Erhardt, *Politische Metaphysik von Solon bis Augustin*, vol. 1: *Die Gottesstadt der Griechen und Römer*, vol. 2: *Die christliche Revolution* (Tübingen, 1959), vol. 3: *Civitas Dei* (Tübingen, 1969).

be built. Certainly, not even his work is free of one-sidedness; it gave rise to misunderstandings that led some astray. But it has proved to be strong enough in its essential core to construct a positive history again after the collapse of the Roman Empire. Augustine's points of departure were so open and broad that they allowed development and deepening, but at the same time they were so large and so pure that one remains on the right path if one follows their direction. But we cannot engage in historical investigations here. Instead, I should like to close by formulating some theses in which it should be possible to see the demarcating line between the essence of Europe and its perversion, between its promise and that which imperils it.

3. Consequences for the Future Path

a. Renunciation of the Belief in Progress

A first thesis must be directed against the myth of progress, which squanders the forces of today on an imaginary tomorrow, thus serving neither the one nor the other. Augustine had regretfully admitted that eternity is not promised to any political structure and that therefore even the Roman Empire could perish, despite its positive achievement, despite its power and even despite its justice. Today also, it is true that no political or cultural form can lay claim to eternity. Even Europe, even the European culture can perish. This does not mean resignation but sobriety. For the essential point in this affirmation is not the assertion of a possible end but the insight that no one can construct the definitive, perfect form of mankind. The future always remains open, because human life lived in common always revolves around human freedom and therefore always has the possibility of failure. But this means that the field of political activity is not the future but the present. The politician is not one who arranges a better world that will arrive at some time or other: rather, his responsibility is that the world today should be good so that it may also be good tomorrow. The so-called better world of tomorrow is a mirage that deprives today of its force and dignity but does not serve tomorrow by so doing. For the idea that one could, by entering into the laws of history, ultimately construct something like earthly paradise as the product of all paths and detours is inimical to freedom and is therefore inhuman. It presupposes that history will one day no longer be based on freedom but on definitive structures. The double paradox of this expectation consists in the fact that one does not wish to free man *for* freedom but *from* his freedom; that one wishes to achieve the absolute—the definitive society— precisely by excluding the absolute criterion—God. Hölderlin was right to say of such endeavors, "Still it is man's desire to make the state his heaven that has made the state hell." [11] Today we know more about how true this is than it was possible for people to see at that time. We must learn to say good-bye to the myth of innerworldly eschatologies. We then serve tomorrow best when we are good today and when we shape today in a spirit of responsibility for what *is* good today and tomorrow.

b. The Priority of Ethics over Politics

This brings us already to a second thesis. We have seen that political activity that revolves around the myth of progress fails to recognize man's freedom, which is called to decision anew in each generation, replacing it with supposed natural laws of history. This essential opposition to freedom in its origin denotes at the same time its antimoral character. Morality is replaced by mechanics. But this is to deny the real foundation of a politics worthy of man. For this foundation is justice, not a justice merely of the group, but an ordered system of law determined by universal moral criteria. Helmut Kuhn has remarked appositely on this: "The construction of the political power structure must go hand in hand with the inner construction, that is, education—and not education for the state (since that would reverse the order of

[11] Cf. H. Kuhn, *Der Staat* (Munich, 1967), 38.

foundation and what is founded), but education to become a person who, as such, is also a citizen of the state." [12] Without the constant endeavor to achieve moral consensus in the great fundamental questions of the human ethos, what is moral has no public power; and without this, it is not possible for men to succeed in living together. Helmut Kuhn has once again formulated precisely the essential point here:

> With the triumph of Hegelianism in Germany, which favored the growth of national socialism and then outlived it, the philosophy of history has taken the place of ethics, and the good has been identified with what is up to date. In an intellectual climate determined by this substitution, the priority of ethics in relation to politics appears to be a moralistic violation of reality, and not even the example of a totally dehumanized politics has been enough to correct this error. [13]

The balance involved here is very subtle. We have said that the state is not the Kingdom of God; the state itself cannot generate morality. It remains a good state precisely when it keeps to these boundaries. But at the same time, it is true that the state lives on the basis of transpolitical foundations and that it can remain good only when these foundations, which it does not itself produce, remain in force. In other words, the state must not make itself into a

[12] Ibid., 85.
[13] Ibid., 29.

religion; it must remain profane and distinguish itself from religion as such. But neither may it decline into the sheer pragmatism of the feasible: it must struggle for the preservation of ethical convictions, since it is only through conviction that ethos can be power and thus indicate the path for the state.[14] Before we draw the concluding consequence of these reflections into a third thesis, their contents must be made somewhat more concrete. "Justice" is the distinguishing mark between state and robber band, as we said above. The robber band too, of course, has its own justice with regard to the group itself. Thus a justice that is more than the regulation of group interests must be subordinate to a universal criterion. In practice, this means for each individual state today that it must subordinate its national common good to the common good of all mankind. It is no longer possible for any state to aim at justice only internally, for itself alone; it takes proper care of the good of its members only when integrated within the totality of mankind. Correct European universality must mean that the individual states transcend and overcome themselves. We must attain today once again what the Greek Aelius Aristides said in his eulogy of Rome in the second century after Christ: "Everything exists for all. No one is a stranger anywhere. . . ." [15]

[14] On the questions addressed here, cf. the important study by H. Schambeck, *Ethik und Staat* (Berlin, 1986).

[15] Cf. Ivánka, 35.

c. Ethics Cannot Renounce the Idea of God

A question opens up the final step of our reflections: What is good for everyone? The mere concept of the universal common good does not suffice; it demands a criterion. The idea of the world-wide common good will become an ethical idea, and thereby worthy of man, only when we learn the Socratic distinction between the good and the things that are good. Once again, we find ourselves referred to the ethos as the foundation of all well-being. The good behind and above all good things has been formulated in the European tradition on a basis that Europe did not give itself but received from a higher tradition: in the Ten Commandments, in which Israel and Christianity, moreover, communicate with the oldest and purest traditions of mankind as a whole. The Ten Commandments also contain the essential core of what the early modern period formulated under the concept of human rights; these in turn are the basis of the distinction between the totalitarian state and the state that imposes limits on itself. The philosopher of religion Georg Picht has shown that the doctrine of human rights is based on the conviction that man is made in the image of God and thus implies the European metaphysics. For this reason, he considers human rights, too, to be something relative, a transitory European phenomenon that cannot serve as the basis of a universal order. Robert Spaemann has objected to this as follows: "Human dignity is an evident postulate to the one who suffers under the degradation of this dignity. And so he must hold to be false any theoretical conviction that would dis- avow this postulate." [16] The suffering of the oppressed becomes here the hermeneutical *locus* in which knowledge of the truth dawns. The consequence that the Munich philosopher draws from these insights seems to me to be irrefutable:

> If Europe does not export its faith, the faith that—as Nietzsche puts it—"God is the truth, that the truth is divine", then it inevitably exports its lack of faith, that is, the conviction that there is no truth and no justice and that the good does not exist. . . . With- out the idea of the unconditional, Europe is nothing more than a geographical concept—besides being a name for the place where the destruction of man began. [17]

I should like to add that Europe will not be able— and will not be permitted—to stop exporting its technology and its rationality. But if this is all it does, then it destroys man's great religious and ethical tra- ditions, destroys the foundations of human existence and subjugates others to a law that will destroy Europe itself too. That would be Eurocentrism in the negative sense of the word. Europe must hand on,

[16] Spaemann, 321f.
[17] Ibid., 322.

not only its rationality, but also the inner origin of this rationality and the foundations that make it meaningful—the recognition of the Logos as the foundation of all things, a glimpse of the truth that is also the criterion of the good. Then Europe will bring together the great traditions of mankind in a process of giving and receiving in which everything belongs to everyone and no one is a stranger to anyone else.

CONCLUSION:
SPEYER—A MIRROR OF EUROPEAN HISTORY

At the end of this attempt to define Europe in its essence and in the perversion of this essence, we must look at the place that has been the occasion for our reflections: at Speyer, now two thousand years old, which is a mirror of Europe in the ups and downs of its history, a mirror of its constructive and destructive forces, a mirror of its hope and of its dangers. Situated at the crossroads between Gaul and Germany, it has experienced both the ascent and the decline of the Roman Empire, at one time as an open space in which the Rhine was not a boundary but a street and a path of encounter, at another time as a fortress in which hostile powers stood opposed to one another. The Gallo-Roman population and the new tribes of the Alemanni and the Franks fused together here during the period of decline and the transition to something new. Then the Irish monks came, not in order to acquire land and power, but to be foreigners with Christ the foreigner and to form the foreign land into a native land in which no one is a foreigner any more. So, in the ninth century, the ancient temple mountain could become the cathedral hill of a new town. The cathedral of the Salic emperors, which came next, attempts to portray in its architecture the unity of Church and empire, the new city of God in which kingship and priesthood are assigned a brotherly relationship to one another. But even while the building is still in process, the investiture conflict draws new boundaries, and so the cathedral, in its finished form, is precisely the testimony that it cannot provide the city of God on earth. The cathedral portrays unity and tension at one and the same time. I shall not pursue further the city's varied history in the age of the Reformation and of absolutism, with the first premonitory signs of European nationalism. One thing is clear: this city has never lived at any stage without looking to what is holy, without the attempt to learn from living together with God how men should live together. So this place may teach us something about the imperfection of all human history, something that not even we can break through. But at the same time, its history teaches us hope, precisely in its moments of decline. We do not know how Europe will look in the third millennium after Christ. But we know what gives support, what is permanent in all millennia, because it is at the same time infinitely open. Europe's greatness is based on a reasonableness in which, despite all that it learns and all that it can do, reason does not forget its highest calling: namely, to be the perception of what is eternal, an organ receptive to God. May the cathedral of Speyer be the symbol of such openness, of such a European spirit, and thereby a guide into a blessed new millennium.

III

A TURNING POINT FOR EUROPE?

Let me begin my reflections on the situation of our
continent with an image. In Israel's history, the collapse of the walls of Jericho appears initially as the
symbol of God's power to shape history but also (and
above all) as the sign that the land has been handed
over to the people who had come from a foreign
country and had wandered for forty years in the
wilderness. It was not military force that threw down
the walls; they collapsed in the presence of a liturgi-
cal procession with God's holy ark and in the presence of the music that accompanied this liturgy.
Naturally, the triumphal element in this moment,
which remained a signal of hope in all subsequent
centuries in the midst of innumerable tribulations,
became obscured again in the history that followed:
life remained exposed and threatened even in the
land they had now at last reached. Inner decadence
gave ever-new strength to external foes, and the fact
that Jericho was finally rebuilt became the sign of a
new dispersal, in which the preceding dissolution of
the spiritual foundations of freedom now simply

became an externally visible event too (cf. 1 Kgs 16:34).

This complex of fulfillment and responsibility, of gift and task, comes spontaneously to mind when one thinks of the political events in the most recent past in Europe, although we naturally ought not to draw inappropriate parallels between the salvation history related in the Bible and events of our own time, thus attributing a false sacral character to these events. It had long seemed incredible to us, men of the enlightenment, that walls should fall down before a procession of people at prayer and before the blasts of their trumpets. But now we have ourselves experienced, if not exactly the same thing, at least something somehow similar: the ideological wall that divided not only Europe but in an invisible manner the whole world everywhere no longer stands as once it did. And it was not thrown down by the power of weapons. Certainly, it was not thrown down simply by means of prayers but through an eruption of the spirit, through processions for freedom that were ultimately de facto stronger than barbed wire and cement. The spirit has shown its power; the trumpet blast of freedom was stronger than the walls that were meant to keep it in check. And even if we ought not to bring God too directly into play here, nevertheless it remains true that faith in him, or at least the question about God, was not insignificant for the sounding-forth of those liberating trumpet blasts.

The fact that closed doors have opened, that separating walls have collapsed and that there is more freedom—these are the consoling and encouraging events of the most recent past of which we ought not to lose sight. They are and remain signposts of and a basis for hope. But neither can we disregard what Israel's history tells us about the course of events after the walls had fallen: namely, that the joy of freedom and of the land possessed in common soon dried up in the troubles of everyday living; that the fact of dwelling in the same land did not in itself knit together a state; and that Israel's growing forgetfulness of God and egotistic misunderstanding of freedom drove it to an inner decadence that ended once again in the loss of freedom (cf. Jg 2:11–23). Freedom is very demanding; it does not keep itself alive, and it ceases to exist precisely when it attempts to be boundless. In other words: the collapse of Marxism does not of itself bring about a free state and a healthy society. History shows again and again the truth of Jesus' image that in the place of one impure spirit who is driven out, seven much worse spirits come when they find the house empty and swept out (Mt 12:43–45 par.). One who abandons Marxism has not thereby automatically found a new foundation on which to base his life. The loss of a hitherto life-supporting ideology can very easily result in nihilism, and that would truly be the reign of the seven worse spirits. But who could ignore the growing tendency to nihilism on the part of the relativism to which we are all exposed today?

Thus we have an urgent question: With what contents can we fill up the intellectual vacuum that has come into being after the failure of the Marxist experiment? On what intellectual foundations can we build a common future in which East and West are joined in a new unity, but also in which North and South find a common path? When we strive to make a diagnosis of our situation and a prognosis of our future tasks and possibilities, this must be done against the criterion of the world as a whole, because today the destiny of each part of mankind is always dependent on the whole, and the decisions of each part have in turn their effect on the whole, so that the only proper way to speak of what is one's own is to speak of the other person. I should therefore like to begin by looking briefly at three fields of tension in today's world politics and economy but also in intellectual confrontations: at the so-called Western world, which has been connecting and blending more and more with what was Eastern Europe after the ideological dogmatism of the East began to evaporate; it will then be necessary to look at the so-called Third World; and finally, we should not fail to give some thought to the third force of the world politics and of the moral-religious drama of our times, namely, the Islamic world, which is emerging ever more strongly.

1. DIAGNOSIS

a. Germany as an Example: The New Western-Eastern World in the Process of Construction

Let us begin with ourselves. On what political forces can we reckon; what tasks confront us, and what dangers must be heeded? It is in Germany that the common European task of this hour is posed with the greatest concreteness and emphasis: in our country, one state from among the previous Eastern states of Europe and one postwar democracy of Western character must grow together to become one single living-space. This process of growing together must at the same time be a growing into a European community in which the nations are no longer autonomous entities that make claims of hegemony vis-à-vis other states but are elements of a greater polymorphic community in which all are related to each other as givers and receivers. Thus two inherited burdens, nationalism and ideological division, must be overcome simultaneously. It will be possible to overcome the economic and political problems posed by the unification of two spheres that have developed in such different ways if a common will undergirds what is done. This common will will withstand the challenges if it is supported by corresponding common convictions. In this sense, the question of intellectual foundations is also the fundamental political question that confronts us today.

Do such foundations exist? There is no doubt that the constitution of the Federal Republic of Germany gives expression to such foundations; it was upon these foundations that the somewhat artificial construction of postwar history was able to grow and regain strength, despite all the tensions. It would be worth investigating more closely the philosophy that stands behind this constitution. Its aim is a legally structured freedom; it knows that freedom and law are not antitheses but rather presuppose each other. It knows that the legislator cannot explain the arbitrary in legal terms and that law is not to be derived simply from statistics. Precisely after the appalling abuse of legal positivism in the Führer's law of the Third Reich, in which injustice had become law and the state had been degraded to the level of a robber band, there existed the awareness that every positive formulation of law must be based on values that elude our manipulation. Only unconditional respect for these values gives the freedom to decide its dignity and its supporting foundations. This is why the Basic Law also knows the limits of the majority principle. And it knows that this inviolability of values, which alone protects the inviolability of the dignity of man and thus his freedom, is based on the fact that these values truly exist and that we bear a responsibility in relation to them. This is expressed very clearly in the preamble to the Basic Law, when we read: "In awareness of its responsibility before God and men . . . the German people . . . has resolved upon this Basic Law of the Federal Republic of Germany." [1] All of this naturally implies that the Basic Law is built on the existence of insights and convictions that themselves do not stand in the law and as such cannot be made into laws but that make laws possible in the first place. The constitution rests on foundations that it cannot prescribe for itself but must presuppose.

This brings us to the critical point of our situation today. To what extent do these foundations still exist? E.-W. Böckenförde has pointed out on occa-

[1] Cf. E. L. Behrendt, *Gott im Grundgesetz. Der vergessene Grundwert "Verantwortung vor Gott"* (Munich, 1980). This remarkable work deserves more attention than it has found hitherto, in my view. A few quotations can serve to indicate the direction of what it says: "That it is the God of the Old and New Testaments to whom our Basic Law appeals as the addressee of responsibility is to be inferred from history, from the ideas of the one who drew up the last constitution, . . . from the concept of responsibility . . . , but above all from the material structure of the norms of this Basic Law itself. This Christian God, and he alone, makes possible and indeed requires tolerance . . ." (318). "Christianity will one day, perhaps soon, have to defend courageously itself and its intellectual foundations. . . . If we lose the adjective 'Christian', then we also lose the God before whom man's responsibility was established and can still be established today. Then it is an unspecific, nonobligatory God that is offered to us. . . . The basis of the responsibility is then an empty shell of a word . . ." (321).

sion that the actual consciousness in society has distanced itself in the intervening period to some extent from these foundations.[2] A new constitutional debate (which is scarcely to be wished for, at least at the moment) would presumably shed a pitiless light on this gradual drying-up of foundations. Even so, what has grown on the basis of the Basic Law is still impressive and strong. Our constitution guarantees a form of life that cannot be condemned as capitalism, since it has produced a social order in which the strong support the weak and in which achievement has its reward but also its responsibility. Accordingly, while our economic order presupposes competition, it does not forget the one who fails to succeed here through no fault of his own. With our legal and social order, we can offer the eastern half of Germany an order of values in which each individual has his dignity, because responsibility before God and men is the decisive basis.

But, as has already been said, we must not overlook the fact that the foundations—ultimately, the recognition of a responsibility before God and

[2] "Ist der deutsche Katholizismus systemkonform? Ein Gespräch mit E.-W. Böckenförde", in *Herder-Korrespondenz* 43 (1989), 262–66. Here Böckenförde shows directly only the changed attitude to the Basic Law in the Church, which leads after initial hesitation to an ever-stronger acceptance and use of the Basic Law; but, indirectly, we also see clearly the development of societal awareness in another direction, which tends rather to lead away from the bases in this world view.

men—are threatened by an insidious erosion and can thereby gradually come to lose their supportive power. A. de Tocqueville pointed out in his studies of democracy in America that the legal forms of this democracy worked because of the unwritten consensus that produced them, that is, on the basis of a Protestant Christian image of man and of the world that stamped the entire structure of life despite or, indeed, precisely because of the strict legal separation between church and state. He showed that the unwritten foundations are much more essential for the continued existence of this democracy than all written law.[3] The situation in our case is not ultimately different. These supportive convictions do not coincide with the doctrines of one particular Christian church, and even today they surely extend far beyond the circle of those who profess allegiance to the churches. Thus one may hope that, thanks to their human evidential character, they can be imparted to the great majority of the East German citizens, too, who are no longer touched by the Christian tradition.

Nevertheless, the extinction of the churches would signify an intellectual landslide on a scale we cannot yet imagine. In my opinion, the events of 1968 and the subsequent development have made clear the direction in which this could go. For the Parisian stu-

[3] Cf. J. Ratzinger, *Kirche, Ökumene und Politik* (Einsiedeln, 1987), 225f.

dent revolution, which launched the phenomenon of
1968, did not crash into the Church from outside:
rather, it erupted from the postconciliar fermen-
tations of Catholicism and from earlier trends in
revolutionary American Protestant theology. The
celebration of the Eucharist on the barricades in Paris
as the fraternity of those struggling for anarchist freedom and as a sign of hope for the political messianism of a new world giving birth to itself in terror
shows the essentially religious—or better, pseudo-
religious—character of what was going on.[4] Nor is it
possible to overlook this theological implication in
the German and Italian terrorism of the 1970s. One
cannot understand the form taken by the Italian terrorism of the early 1970s without the inner crises and
ferments of postconciliar Catholicism;[5] in Germany,
it drew its nourishment especially from the student
parishes, here with a more American and Protestant
coloring.

The political messianism and the violent zealotry
that accompanied it have subsided in the meantime.
It had already lost its credibility even before the

[4] The study by M. J. Le Guillou, O. Clément and J. Bosc,
Évangile et révolution (Paris, 1968), written directly under the
impact of the events, remains still the most impressive contribution to this question.

[5] Cf. M. Cuminetti, *Il dissenso cattolico in Italia* (Milan, 1983);
A. Socci and R. Fontolan, *1974 Tredici anni della nostra storia 1987*
(Milan, 1988).

debacle of real socialism. In the course of its actions, it became obvious that this could be neither the updating of Christianity nor the threshold of a better world; it became clear that the message of Jesus offers no basis for these applications. But the wounds received then have remained; they appear in various forms. The increasing power of drugs is a sign of an emptiness in the soul to which nothing more remains after the loss of ideological promises. Life has become boring and empty. Last autumn, the Italian government began an advertising campaign against the spread of drugs, in which pictures of the cheerful life of young people were shown, followed by the slogan: "This is what life is like. Don't burn it up with drugs." But could these pictures, in which young people laugh and joke, be truly convincing? *Is* life like that? Do not the films that then follow, with images full of cruelty, hatred, anger and disappointments, show that life is quite different? Is this not real life? We have been told with great thoroughness that the unscathed world does not exist, and modern film-makers appear to take it as honesty when they show man almost always as base and coarse. But both are distorted images of life. Life is not only happiness and games: it is pain, temptation and failure. And yet in all this it is beautiful if it is supported by love and possesses a hope that transcends the present moment. If we cannot show a picture of life in which even pain, hardship and death are meaningful and belong to a larger whole, then we cannot rehabilitate human existence. This is surely the chief question to which we must give an answer today: Is it really good to be alive and to be a human being? We cannot answer this question unless there is a goodness that is bestowed on each individual and is stronger than all our failure.

The ideological terrorism of the 1970s has divided today in two directions: on the one side, we have the "withdrawal symptoms" caused by the loss of ideology—the desert of nihilism, in which consolation is sought in drugs. On the other side, we can observe the transition from violent activity to criminal organizations, which no longer need any ideology. The drug cartel in Colombia is recruited in part from former ideological combatants. But we must also ask: How are things with religion? Has it regenerated itself? Where does the path lead?

I would say that there are without doubt signs of regeneration that permit us to hope—young movements in which a great power of faith is at work, a convincing ethical seriousness and a readiness to commit one's own life that is admirable. Such movements can be a yeast that gives fresh vital force and authenticity to the humane values of the Gospel that mark our constitution. But we cannot deceive ourselves about the continuing exodus from the churches or about the internal crises that continue to shake them. On the whole, one can observe a progressive dissolution of religion in our society, in a twofold direction. We have already met the first of these directions when we looked at the events of 1968: politics becomes religion, and religion turns into a political passion. Faith in the transcendence and the eternal destiny of man decays: it appears to be without rational foundation and valueless for shaping life in this world. But what remains is the expectation of unconditional salvation. The experience of being unredeemed, of alienation, becomes stronger, and fulfillment—which cannot lie beyond and is not given as a gift of any grace—must now be realized through one's own action in this world. But this ties an expectation to politics that politics cannot satisfy. Religion that has turned into politics makes excessive demands of politics and thereby becomes a source of the disintegration of man and of society.

The other form of the dissolution of religion leads into an area that can be called "gnosticism", in terms of the history of religions, and that is often classed today under the label of esotericism. It covers many varied forms of religious substitutes with often strange mixtures of the rational and the irrational. Occultism and magic become attractive; it is always a matter of a religion that does not demand faith but that leads into deeper strata of existence along the path of rites and psychological practices, conveys the feeling of breaking through barriers and of liberation, and supplies from hidden depths a power against the forces that threaten our life. In the search for a tech-nique of redemption, recourse is had to non-European forms of religion that do not hold man in the tiresome balance of faith but offer him practical forms of self-redemption. Much is said today about the secularization of our society. This is correct in the sense that religion withdraws into the private realm. But it does not disappear: it only changes its form and thereby, of course, its inner essence too. If one looks at the marketplace of religions spread out before us today, one can clearly observe both their presence in the transformation and the change in the essence of the religious phenomenon. The essence of the Christian faith, considered from the perspective of the phenomenology of religions, consists in its uniting man's primal religious drive in a subtle syn-thesis with a rationally formed turning to the one God who is seen to be the reason at work in the ori-gin of all things and as creative love. The conse-quence of this is an ethos that listens to the reason of creation and finds in this an echo of the reason of the Creator. This synthesis of understanding, will and feeling is not easy; it is always in danger of being dis-solved in one direction or the other. Beyond the sphere of Christianity, this same tension also deter-mines the drama of religious history. Almost all reli-gions know the one God, the one origin of the world who imparts meaning, behind the divine pow-ers of the world. Even for polytheism, it is clear in general terms that the gods are not the plural of God, because God does not exist in the plural. He is unique. Although the gods are designated by the same name, they are powers of a lower rank. But, again and again in the history of religions, this one God disappears from worship and from concrete religious conduct. He is too distant and, above all, he is not dangerous, either because he is only good, the absolutely good one who therefore does evil to no one, or else because one thinks that he is not concerned about what happens to men, who are too lowly for him. Thus worship is directed, not to the only good one, from whom in any case nothing is to be feared, but to the many ambiguous powers who concretely beset our life and with whom one must come to terms.[6] I would call this chronic defection from the one God to the many ambiguous powers in the history of religions paganism in the qualitative sense of the word. In this sense, we are threatened today by a new paganism in the enlightened Western world, but also for this reason in all other cultures too. The man who excludes the one good foundation of all things as too distant, too uncertain and too unimportant, so that he may turn instead to the powers that lie closer at hand, abases himself. The decomposition of the Christian synthesis facing us

[6] I have attempted to describe these connections in my contribution to the Festschrift for K. Rahner, *Gott in Welt* (1964), 2:287–305: "Der christliche Glaube und die Weltreligionen".

must ultimately also lead to a disintegration of man himself.

b. The "Third World"

Before we draw conclusions from this attempt at a diagnosis of today's Western-Eastern world, we must first look at the two other spheres that are making their mark on world history at present: the so-called Third World and the world of Islam. As far as the Third World is concerned, the fall of the invisible (or sometimes very visible) wall that divided the world everywhere is beyond doubt great progress, since the antagonism of East and West had been projected onto the whole rest of the world. Countries lacking the necessities of life were supplied with refined weapons systems and were repeatedly designated as the arena of vicarious wars in which both power blocs strove to assert their relative superiority. A political messianism was taught that tore these countries apart from within and divided them into hostile combat positions; violence was unleashed on all sides, among the defenders of conservative ideologies no less than among the revolutionary groups on the left. These phenomena have not simply disappeared under the sign of the growing reconciliation between East and West through the disintegration of Marxist ideology, especially because their societal causes continue to exist: but there are increasing possibilities of finding rational political solutions. This is an extremely positive process; a politics free of ideology must show itself here to be an ethically responsible politics, demonstrating that the lack of a fully developed ideology does not mean the absence of the ethical values that generate the force to achieve reconciliation and the nonviolent overthrow of the structures of injustice.

The opportunity confronting us makes high demands on our moral and religious strength. Only if we hold firm here will the new Western-Eastern world itself be able to master its fundamental problems. The model of development that has hitherto been practiced in the West is inadequate here.[7] It was unsatisfactory even without the additional burden of the East-West conflict. Certainly one cannot make the West alone responsible for the fact that the economic distance between North and South did not diminish but rather increased in the last decades.

[7] The interview given by P. Merz to the *Herder-Korrespondenz* 44 (1990), 519–26, "Entwicklungszusammenarbeit nach dem Ende des Ost-Westkonflikts", is instructive on the present state of the debate about development. Despite all the important acknowledgments and insights here, one is surprised at the continuing almost total failure to take up questions of morals and world view. When, for example, the achievements and successes up to the present are defended by a reference to the increase in life expectancy from 46 to 62 years, and in literacy from 43 to 60 percent, one must ask what increased life expectancy means when the contents of life are lost, and what literacy means in view of the loss of meaning.

There are also internal causes in the Third World itself, especially the often prevalent corruption and, in not a few places, the lack of a work ethic. But this already brings us to the dubious point of the Western form of aid: namely, the belief that one could prescind altogether from ethical problems and bring about in a purely mechanical fashion the construction of modern economies while bypassing the existing ethical and social systems. Even the churches, who really ought to have known better, often succumbed to this materialistic illusion. Many of their emissaries were of the opinion that one must first spread the blessing of prosperity, and then one could also go on to speak of God. But this is a fundamentally false application of the axiom *"primum vivere, deinde philosophari"* ("first let us live, then let us philosophize"). For the core of faith in God and of its ethical force is not a philosophy that lies within the reach only of those who have enough for their life: rather, it is the precondition of life, it *is* life. The young African intellectuals who studied at European universities acquired for the most part only an academic knowledge completely devoid of the ethical and the religious. All that remained to them was the choice between positivism and Marxism, but neither of these two philosophies is capable of building up a society in which freedom and justice are connected in a meaningful way. Here lie the deepest roots of the anger that is spreading in the Third World today against Europe and America in particular. Certainly, this anger is also (and initially) caused by the difference in prosperity between the two halves of the earth. It is clear, however, that the existence of a deeper wound plays a role in the passionate recourse to African culture and religion, to the Latin American or Asian identity, that we observe today: the consciousness that one's own soul has been trampled upon, that one has been hurt in one's inmost depths, and that with all the gifts one received, one has been robbed of one's dignity and of what allows one to live in the deepest sense. In this connection, it is interesting that the rebellion in Latin American today against the European culture and tradition, after the Marxist model ran its course, is orchestrated with two new motifs. The memory of the five hundred years that have elapsed since Europe invaded America should remind one of the oppression of the Indian cultures, which one would now like to discover anew as the true soul of South America. Besides this, there is a passionate turning to the Blacks who were carried off to America and the lamentation over the loss of their cultural and religious identity. Both movements identify Europe with Christianity; to this extent, they are also a rebellion against Christianity as the religion of the overlords and as an alienating power—a rebellion that paradoxically finds its strongest spokesmen among theologians, who attempt in this way to give a new form to the theme of liberation. But in Africa, too, there is an ever-stronger fight not only against Christianity but especially against the inculturation of the Christian faith in African culture as a form of alienation; and there is a new search for their own religious tradition, though this has lost its roots and can continue to exist in a fruitful manner only if it arises anew within the Christian sphere.

Contemporary with these processes, we can observe a stronger tendency to dissolve the one Church into sects; not only sects with an essentially Christian character, but sects of increasingly syncretistic construction, which blend together elements of very diverse provenance to make new forms. Particularly noticeable is the advance of sects of North American origin throughout Latin America, whose traditional Catholic character has been replaced in many places by a new religious pluralism. The reasons for this revolutionary turn of events are still very far from clear. Many factors work together: the greater mobility and dynamism of the new religious groups; active and sometimes aggressive missionary methods, linked to social and economic advantages; an insufficient evangelization on the Catholic side. Besides this, two reasons are mentioned again and again, whose validity, of course, would have to be investigated in greater depth. On the one hand, a one-sided political pastoral care has created in many places a religious vacuum that is filled by the sects, who respond to the unsatisfied religious hunger precisely of poor people. The latter commonly have no use for the ideology of a better future world and have to suffer the most under the violent actions that supposedly lead to it. On the other hand, one hears again and again the hypothesis that the propaganda of the sects is being promoted by the United States, which supposedly hopes to achieve thereby a structural harmonization of the southern half of America with its own mentality, with favorable repercussions in political and economic structures. Such expectations, of course, could prove to be deceptive, because an opposition against what is foreign is now being aroused against new forms of religious dependency at the same time, and it is not possible to foresee the internal developments of the religious consciousness after the fragmentation of Christianity. This picture would be all too incomplete, however, if one failed to point also to the impressive renaissance of Catholicism in many places, with a rediscovery of both its religious depths and its social responsibility under the challenges of the present day precisely in Latin America, so that it is thereby also able to inspire enthusiasm and give formation.

c. The Islamic World

Finally, we must turn our attention briefly to the Islamic world; naturally, it is not possible here to give even an approximate description of this multi-faceted reality. I should like only to look critically at one of the catchwords in the present debate, which is often offered as a general key to under-standing today's course of events: "fundamentalism". If we begin by ascertaining briefly the basis of the contemporary renaissance of the Islamic world, two causes strike us at once. First, there is the eco-nomic, and thereby also the political and military, strengthening of the Islamic countries through the importance that oil has attained in international pol-itics. But whereas the economic advance in the West has led in general to a dilution of religious substance, in the Islamic world, the new economic strength is linked to a new religious self-awareness; it is of course true that religion, culture and politics stand together in Islam in an inseparable unity. This new religious self-awareness and the attitudes result-ing from it are often termed "fundamentalism" in the West today. In my view, this is the inappropri-ate transfer of a concept from American Protestant-ism into a wholly different world, and this does not help us truly to understand what is going on. Funda-mentalism, according to the word's original mean-ing, is a tendency that arose in Protestant America in the nineteenth century as a protest against evolution-ism and biblical criticism. It attempted to supply a firm Christian foundation against both of these through the defense of the absolute inerrancy of

Scripture.[8] There doubtless exist analogies to this
attitude in other spiritual worlds too, but one falls
victim to a false simplification if one changes analogies into an identification. This catchword has been
made into an all-too-simple key that permits us to
divide the world into two halves, a good half and a
bad half. The series of supposed fundamentalisms
has in the meantime passed from the Protestant
over the Catholic to the Islamic and the Marxist
fundamentalisms. The differences in content go
utterly unheeded; one is a fundamentalist if one has
firm convictions, for this is viewed as something
that provokes conflicts and is opposed to progress.
In contrast, the "good" is the doubt that takes up
the battle against old certainties—that is, every
modern undogmatic or antidogmatic movement.

But one cannot truly give an explanation of the
world while bypassing the contents so simply, merely
using a formal division into categories. In my view,
one ought to abandon completely talk of Islamic fundamentalism, because it does more to conceal very
different processes under a simplifying label than to

8 S. E. Ahlstrom, "Fundamentalismus", in *RGG* 2:1178f.,
offers precise information and a detailed bibliography. The article
"Fundamentalismus" by J. Niewadomski, in H. Gasper, J. Müller
and F. Valentin (eds.), *Lexicon der Sekten* (Herder, 1990), 330–36,
is rich in materials but yields, in my view, to the temptation to
broaden the concept in such a way that it becomes a slogan of
ideological conflict, losing its own inherent outlines.

shed light on them.[9] It seems to me that one must make a distinction between the *starting point* of the new Islamic awakening and then the different *forms* that this takes. As for the starting point, it seems to me very significant that the first indications of the turning point in Iran were attacks on American movies. The Western way of life with its moral permissiveness was felt to be an attack on their own identity and on the dignity of their own way of life. At the height of its power, the Christian world had evoked a sense of underdevelopment and of doubt in the Islamic way, at least in the educated circles of the Islamic world; but now contempt grows at the sight of how morality and religion are relegated to the merely private sphere, at the sight of a public life that is shaped in such a way that only religious and moral agnosticism counts as acceptable. The power with which this way of life was officially forced upon them, above all through American cultural exportation, so that it should appear to be the only normal thing, was experienced more and more as an attack on the depths of their own being. The reason why it

[9] The concept of "Islamic fundamentalism" has been criticized recently by J. Reissner in a lecture at the 1989 meeting of the Görres-Gesellschaft; cf. *Jahres- und Tagungsbericht* of the Gessellschaft (Cologne, 1990), 176f. "Thus, what we call 'Islamic fundamentalism' is not to be interpreted by religious science as a 'return to the Middle Ages' but as the attempt to confront the questions of the present day while preserving Islam's claim to validity" (177).

was not the atheistic Soviet Union but rather the religiously tolerant America, which has indeed a strongly religious character, that was seen and combatted as the personification of evil is connected with this collision between a morally agnostic culture and a structure of life in which nation, culture, morality and religion appear as an indivisible totality.

The concrete forms taken by this new self-awareness are varied. An obsession with the letter of religious traditions is often bound to a political and military fanaticism in which religion is seen directly as a path to earthly power. The Islamic tradition itself could easily suggest this instrumentalization of the religious energies for the political field. In connection with the phenomenon of Palestinian opposition, a revolutionary interpretation of Islam has developed that comes very close to Christian theologies of liberation and has facilitated the coalescence of Western European, Marxist-inspired terrorism and Islamic terrorism. What is superficially called Islamic fundamentalism found no difficulty in associating itself with socialist ideas of liberation: Islam is presented as the true bearer of the struggle of oppressed peoples for freedom. It is along this line that R. Garaudy, for example, found his way from Marxism to Islam, in which he sees the bearer of revolutionary forces against the dominant capitalism. In contrast, as deeply religious a ruler as King Hassan of Morocco has recently expressed his profound anxiety about the future of Islam: one understanding of Islam that sees its essence in devotion to God struggles with a political-revolutionary interpretation in which the religious element becomes part of a cultural chauvinism and is thereby ultimately subordinated to the political. The confrontation with this many-faceted phenomenon should not be taken too lightly. The Islam that is sure of itself has to a large extent a greater fascination for the Third World than a Christianity that is in a state of inner decay.

2. The Task

a. State and Society

What is the consequence of all this for society and Church here? What must we do? In the case of society, we ought to pay greater attention than hitherto, especially because of the experiences of the last two decades, to what Horkheimer and Adorno have called the dialectics of the Enlightenment. By this is meant the "total self-destruction of the Enlightenment",[10] which occurs where the Enlightenment

---

[10] M. Horkheimer and T. W. Adorno, *Dialektik der Aufklärung* (Fischer-Taschenbuch 6144). I take this quotation and the following from the noteworthy essay by H. Staudinger, "Christentum und Aufklärung", in *Forum Katholische Theologie* 6 (1990), 190–206, particularly 199.

absolutizes itself and wishes to know only what is calculable and explicable but denies or relegates to the merely private sphere everything that is not readily at its disposal. In other words, no society will long survive if in its public structure it is built agnostically and materialistically and wishes to permit anything else to exist only below the threshold of the public. If we wish to summarize succinctly today's problem and the challenge it poses, I would say that it lies in the double dissolution of the moral realm, which seems to have been making inexorable progress up to now: in the privatization of morality, on the one hand, and in its reduction, on the other hand, to the calculation of what will be successful, of what promises better chances of survival. This makes a society an immoral society in its public and communal essence—or, in other words, a society that attaches no value to what really gives dignity to man and constitutes him as a human person.

Thus, the first and most urgent imperative seems to me the renewed recognition of the place of the moral sphere in its inviolability and dignity. The distinguishing mark of man is that he not only acknowledges his physical inability to do something as a limit but also freely respects the moral prohibition against doing something as an equally binding and real limit. He is free, and he is a human person, when he not only bows to the law of necessity but also acknowledges the law of freedom as the sphere that determines him; then, he can go in the opposite direction, breaking through the limits of what is physically necessary, or attempting to push these limits farther, without imperiling himself or creation. The inherent worth of a society is seen in the values it counts worth protecting. A concern for physical integrity, which sometimes seems quite pathological, is characteristic of our society. There may indeed be something true involved here, but the frantic anxiety and the distortion of perspectives that can be observed here point rather to that "radicalized mythical anxiety" that Horkheimer has shown to be a mark of an Enlightenment that is leading into positivism.[11] Over against this pathological concern for the protection of our physical integrity stands a widely diffused indifference to the moral integrity of the human person, which seems worthy of no praise but is rather scorned as hypocrisy or absurdity by the rationalist-turned-positivist. But this is actually the negation of man as man, the negation of freedom and of human dignity. We will not long survive like that, and we certainly cannot give effective help to anyone else.

Naturally, there are understandable reasons for the relegation of the moral dimension to the private sphere: fear of moral constraint, of manipulation by the state, of ideological intolerance. But these fears are essential principles for a lawgiver only because of

[11] Ibid., 13; Staudinger, 201.

their inherent moral value: the acknowledgment of the conscience and of its own right, the acknowledgment of the limits placed on the state's discretion, and so on. To this extent, a bit of morality has been made a part of the public order, and the state is no longer totally uninvolved in moral-religious issues. But why is it that we can really attach a public obligation only to the setting of these boundary lines? They are important, but they are not the sum total of what a society needs in order to survive. Despite all the Christian self-criticism, which has become ever more intense and radical since the Enlightenment, we ought to find our way back to an awareness of the great moral tradition of Christianity, to the pre- or meta-dogmatic core (so to speak) of its moral constants, and to recognize this as our spiritual and intellectual identity, on the basis of which we can live—as this was still presupposed in the Basic Law of 1949. If we do not rediscover a part of our Christian identity, we shall not be able to meet the challenge of this hour.

b. The Church

But what ought the Church or the churches to do in this connection? I would reply: They should, first of all, truly be themselves for once. They must not allow themselves to be downgraded to a mere means for making society moral, as the liberal state wished; still less should they want to justify themselves through the usefulness of their social works. The more the Church aims directly at what in her ought to be something "of itself extraneous", so to speak, the more she will fail in this attempt. It is typical that in the Church today, the more she understands herself first and foremost as an institute for social progress, the more the social vocations dry up—the calls to serve the old, the sick, children, and so forth, vocations that flourished so much when the Church still looked essentially to God. One could say that this is a purely empirical proof of the truth of Jesus' *logion*: "Seek first the kingdom of God and his righteousness, and all the rest will be given you" (Mt 6:33). Horkheimer and Adorno, with the clear sight of the outsider, have denounced the attempt by theologians to sneak past the core of the faith, removing the provocatory character of the Trinity and life beyond death as well as of the biblical narratives by reducing these to the level of symbols. They tell us that when theologians bracket off dogma, what they say has no validity; they bow to that "fear of the truth" in which the spiritual and intellectual decline of the present day has its roots.[12] No, one cannot save the Church in this way. She must first do decisively what is her very own, she must fulfill the task

[12] For criticism of theology, see, for example, T. W. Adorno, *Stichworte* (edition suhrkamp 347), 25 (Staudinger, 203, with further references); on the "fear of the truth": *Dialektik der Aufklärung*, 3 (Staudinger, 201).

in which her identity is based: to make God known and to proclaim his Kingdom. Precisely thus, and only thus, does that sphere of the soul come into existence in which the moral dimension regains its existence, far beyond the circle of those who believe.

Irrespective of this, the Church must accept her responsibility for society in various ways, not least by attempting to make herself comprehensible; she must give insight into what belongs to God and into the moral sphere that results from this. She must convince, for it is only by convincing that she opens up space for what has been entrusted to her; and this can be made accessible only along the path of freedom, which means via reason, will and emotion. The Church must be ready to suffer. She must prepare space for the divine, not through power but through spirit, not through institutional strength but through witness, through love, life and suffering: and in this way she must help society to find its moral identity.

Goethe once termed the struggle between belief and unbelief the great theme of world history, picking up a theme of Augustine's philosophy of history. Augustine himself, of course, expressed this differently: he sees in world history the struggle between two kinds of love, love for self, which goes as far as despising God, and love for God, which goes as far as despising oneself. Today, we can perhaps formulate this in still another way: history is marked by the confrontation between love and the inability to love,

that devastation of the soul that comes when the only
values man is able to recognize at all as values and
realities are quantifiable values. The capacity to love,
that is, the capacity to wait in patience for what is
not under one's own control and to let oneself
receive this as a gift, is suffocated by the speedy
fulfillments in which I am dependent on no one but
in which I am never obliged to emerge from my
own self and thus never find the path into my own
self. This destruction of the capacity to love gives
birth to lethal boredom. It is the poisoning of man.[13]

---

[13] Cf. T. Goritschewa, *Von Gott zu reden ist gefährlich* (Freiburg, 1984), 21, in the description of the intellectual situation
before her conversion: "To be more clever than the others, more
capable, stronger—that was my goal. But no one had ever told
me that the highest goal does not lie in overtaking and beating
others but in loving." The antithesis is very finely presented in
fiction in M. Ende's fairytale novel *Momo* (Stuttgart, 1973). I am
thinking of the scene where one of the grey gentlemen offers
Momo the whole arsenal of technically perfect dolls, and, when
Momo objects, "I don't believe . . . that one can love them",
replies: "The only thing . . . that counts in life is succeeding in
something, becoming something, possessing something. If you
have more success, if you become more and have more than the
others, you get everything else quite automatically: friendship,
love, honor and so on . . . " (93f.). So also the other scene where
Master Hora, the mysterious administrator of time, speaks of the
dead human time, whose steamy bell-jar makes one sick: "At the
beginning, one does not notice much of this. One day, one has
no more desire to do anything. Nothing is interesting, one is
bored. . . . One becomes quite indifferent and grey. . . . There is

If he were to have his way, man would be destroyed, and the world with him. In this drama, we should not hesitate to oppose the omnipotence of the quantitative and to take up our position on the side of love. This is the decision that the present hour demands of us.

---

no longer any anger, any enthusiasm, one can no longer rejoice, no longer mourn. . . . Then it has become cold, and one can no longer love anything or anyone. . . . This sickness is called: lethal boredom."